I Had a Dr IBM Could Be # 1 Again

I0008848

Big Blue'sJob Is To Be # 1!

*IBM's marketing troubles with its most loyal constituency can end
tomorrow if Big Blue chooses again to be the # 1 technology
company in the world. It's up to IBM!.*

B R I A N W. K E L L Y

Copyright © 2016
Author Brian W. Kelly
Title: *I Had a Dream that IBM Could Be # 1 Again*
Publisher: Brian P. Kelly

All rights reserved: No part of this book may be reproduced or transmitted in any form, or by any means, electronic or mechanical, including photocopying, recording, scanning, faxing, or by any information storage and retrieval system, without permission from the publisher, LETS GO PUBLISH, in writing.

Disclaimer: Though judicious care was taken throughout the writing and the publication of this work so that the information contained herein is accurate, there is no expressed or implied warranty that all information in this book is 100% correct. Therefore, neither LETS GO PUBLISH, nor the author accepts liability for any use of this work.

Trademarks: A number of products and names referenced in this book are trade names and trademarks of their respective companies. For example, Power i and AS/400 are trademarks of the IBM Corporation and Windows is a trademark of Microsoft Corporation.

Referenced Material: The information in this book has been obtained through personal and third party observations and copious reading over many years. Where unique information has been provided or extracted from other sources, those sources are acknowledged within the text of the book itself. Thus, there is no formal footnotes or bibliography section.

Published by: LETS GO PUBLISH!
                 Brian P. Kelly, Publisher
                 P.O Box 621
                 Wilkes-Barre, PA 18703
                 brian@brianpkelly.com
                 www.letsgopublish.com

Library of Congress Copyright Information Pending

Book Cover Design by Michele Thomas

ISBN Information: The International Standard Book Number (ISBN) is a unique machine-readable identification number, which marks any book unmistakably. The ISBN is the clear standard in the book industry. 159 countries and territories are officially ISBN members. The Official ISBN For this book is: **996245499** and the ISBN 13 is **9780996245494**

The price for this work is : $14.95 USD

10   9   8   7   6   5   4   3   2

Release Date: August 2016

Dedication

To My Wonderful Neighbors

Angel Mrs. Mercedes Leighton
Mrs. Jeanne and Mr. Joseph Elinsky
Mr. Joseph and Mrs. Carolyn Langan
Mrs. Carol and Mr. John Anstett
Dr. Dwaraki Bai and Dr. Haragopal Penugonda
Angel Mrs. Maxine and Angel Mr. Simon H. Coblentz
Mr. Ozzie Kroll

The day that my neighbors, who are all professionals and business people in their day jobs, understand the elegance and desirability of the IBM AS/400 (now known as IBM Power System with IBM i) from having heard IBM's message, is the day that the AS/400's chances of survival as a relevant business computer begin to increase.

Acknowledgments

I would like to thank many, many people for helping me in this effort to produce my 67th book.

To all the people that I have ever mentioned in the Acknowledgments of any book, I continue to appreciate your contributions. For those new to the experience of helping me bring in my book projects and /or who help me in my life, I want to thank you all from the bottom of my heart.

Please check out www.letsgopublish.com Acknowledgments to read the latest version of what once was the largest acknowledgments in the world, though the rigors of the Guinness Book were too time consuming for LGP to apply.

So, please go to www.letsgopublish.com and choose acknowledgments so you can see your name in print or you can see who helped in the production of this book.

You are listed online and if not please send me a spirited, yet irritated response. I do appreciate your great work in my publishing efforts.

God Bless all the helpers!

Thank you so very much!

Table of Contents

Preface:

This book is about a dream that I had not too long ago during a period in which I had written a number of IBM books. The dream was real. I woke up trying to figure out how I could take the ideas in the dream and present them to the IBM Company. This book will be given to IBM for its internal use. I hope it will help.

So, this dream actually happened to me. As a 23+ year IBMer nobody in IBM ever called me to ask if I had regretted retiring. I am glad to be on my own but I still reflect on what could have been. I even dreamabout it.

My dream was about what I had always hoped that IBM would do with all of its business opportunities instead of permitting more than its share to go south.

I believe that IBM can make my dream and the dream of many other IBMers and IBM rooters, come true. It is a dream about what IBM needs to do to become # 1 again in the Information Technology Industry.

I Had a Dream that IBM Could Be # 1 Again

I hope that at the very least, along with learning a number of things, you enjoy reading this book. I sure have enjoyed writing it. IBM can again be #1 and I would be pleased to help.

Brian W. Kelly
Wilkes-Barre, Pennsylvania

About the Author

Brian W. Kelly retired as an Assistant Professor in the Business Information Technology (BIT) program at Marywood University, where he also served as the IBM i and midrange systems technical advisor to the IT faculty. Kelly has designed, developed, and taught many college and professional courses. He is also a contributing technical editor to a number of IT industry magazines, including "The Four Hundred" and "Four Hundred Guru" published by IT Jungle. On the patriotic side, you once could find a patriotic Kelly article at www.conservativeactionalerts.com. This site no longer functions but the articles are still hosted at www.brianwkelly.com

Kelly is a former IBM Senior Systems Engineer and he has been a candidate for US Congress and the US Senate from Pennsylvania. He has an active information technology consultancy. He is the author of 55 books and numerous articles. Kelly is a frequent speaker at National Conferences, and other technical conferences.

Over the past twenty years, Brian Kelly has become one of America's most outspoken and eloquent technical authors. Besides this book, his titles about IBM include *Chip Wars*; *Can the AS/400 Survive IBM?* *Thanks You IBM:* The story of how IBM helped today's technology billionaires and millionaires gain their vast fortunes, *The All-Everything Machine, The All-Everything Operating System, Whatever happened to the IBM AS/400? Besides these,* many other Kelly books are available at www.bookhawkers.com

Endorsed by the Independence Hall Tea Party in 2010, Kelly, a Democrat, ran for Congress against a 13-term Democrat and, took no campaign contributions, spent enough to buy signs and T-shirts, and as a virtual unknown, he captured 17% of the vote—www.briankellyforcongress.com. Kelly then supported Republican challenger Lou Barletta, a conservative leader on immigration policy, and helped him win a resounding victory in the general election.

Chapter 1   I Had a Dream—Really!

Can dreams come true?

I had a dream. I am not kidding. It was less than a week ago after I had prepared my newest book, *Thank You IBM* for sale on Kindle. IBM was on my mind for some reason. With 23 years of employment at IBM, I have a lot of recollections of Big Blue that come back to me too often when I am sleeping. This was a nice IBM dream. It had an impact on me.

It was unlike some IBM dreams that I have had in the past. For example, one time I forgot to bring my slides to a sales meeting and woke up just in time. Another time, I forgot that I was going to be called on at the Branch Meeting by the Regional Manager. Then of course was the time that I really did not know what I was talking about when I was to introduce a new IBM product that I had yet to understand to my peers.

My most recent dream, thankfully was actually a nice dream. Unlike most dreams, this dream has a shot at coming true. But, that will be up to the IBM Corporation. It is about Big Blue getting to the top once again.

I was not afraid of IBM ever. However, I did not want to mess up in front of peers, customers or management. IBM was a great company to work for—especially in the beginning for me when Thomas Watson, Jr. was our Chairman and CEO (cover pictures).

On my first day of work at the IBM Office in Utica, NY on June 23, 1969, everybody was at the office for a meeting.

There were more donuts than I had ever seen and the coffee was first-class out of this world.

Everybody at the meeting in Utica looked more important than I felt. IBM in Utica had seven new hires beginning this day and we all got to say hello to our new peers. We were not given much time because the meeting purpose was not to greet us but to discuss a new way that IBM was going to conduct business in the future.

IBMers who you do not know always seem to have an important look about them. I never felt that I looked like a real IBMer but over time, I knew that I was as good as any other Systems Engineer at my job. At this meeting, my first in the "IBM Blue uniform", however, I was daunted. I was trying to figure out just how I fit in—in a Utica, NY IBM Sales Office.

All my new peers looked like me when they were munching those great donuts or Danish but when they commented at this meeting, I knew they were all special people and smart as a whip for sure. I did not even know the meaning of all the words they were using and though I was a Data Processing Major, I knew little of the jargon. I became convinced that my IBM career would be a challenge but I was ready for it.

In my dream after 23 years of IBM, and a lot of time teaching and running my own tech business, I was thinking about how special it was to be part of that IBM group and many more groups of IBMers over the years. To be favored with a job with IBM was impressive unto itself.

I dreamt that IBM could be #1 again and part of the secret was for the company to give its employees the great feeling of satisfaction and worth that I had while working for The International Business Machines Corporation. If IBM could do that, it would be a great start to get back to # 1.

A lot of things came to mind about why it was that I loved the IBM Company as I did and why I still have a picture of

Thomas Watson, Jr. hanging on the wall in my Sun Room. He is my favorite IBMer of all time next to his Dad, Thomas Sr. Lou Gerstner comes in #2. Watson was the Chairman of IBM on June 23, 1969, my first day of work for the company.

The Chairman of the board and CEO was not at our meeting but we got to see him in a prerecorded videotape which was viewed by all branches that day. We can't bring either Watson back for IBM today but if that Watson spirit could be infused again into the company, it would go a long way to bringing my favorite company back to # 1. It is amazing how hard and how smart people will work in the right setting. When I worked for IBM in the early years, losing was never an option. Winning was exhilarating.

IBM Focus to get to the top

IBM getting to the top begins with IBM becoming serious about becoming #1 again. Nobody will ever be #1 if they think being #2 or # 22 is OK! The right plan will flow from wanting and creating the specifics in a plan to be # 1. Adding some Watson beliefs to the mix would be major ingredients to long-term success.

I'd sure like to help in whatever way I can and so would a number of pundits and ex IBMers and former customers from IBM's good days. We know how good IBM can be. Many of us still talk about what IBM could do to be a better company. Everything is possible. Believing that IBM can be # 1 again is the first and most important step. Acting in spirit like the old IBM is a close #2.

IBM can come back to the top if it changes its ways. Sometimes we all can learn about how we once behaved if we can see our actions in a mirror. A lot of this book is that mirror for IBM. There are some great mirrors to look at such as when IBM was a fledgling company. The mirrors would be a great reflection of IBM until some time after the end of the Watson era. Then, there are some bad mirrors for IBM to examine that we would not want IBM to repeat on its way back to the top—or Big Blue will never get there.

I worked for this great company for twenty-three years and then for another 20 years, I was an IT professor and an information technology consultant. I was an expert in a number of IBM products over those many years. From so many years on the job, I also became an expert in IBM as a company, and because of both experiences, I am confident that I am qualified to offer IBM many suggestions for improvement.

If we could only bring the dead back to life, I am convinced that if a Watson ran IBM from 1971 until today, IBM would be a $500 billion dollar company and there would be enough change left over to make me even a regular guy like me into a millionaire. Obviously no Watson will be returning to IBM any time soon so the company must look elsewhere for a great top manager. Another Lou Gerstner would not be too bad of a choice but the best approach would be to outline the list of Watson characteristics and keep looking until we find the right CEO and Chairperson.

If Virginia Rometty, the current CEO happens to be that person then so be it. She would have to read all of the Watson books available along with all of the Watson recommendations for managers and employees to be able to move IBM into # 1 again. She would need a special type of training that focused on excellence in all activities, not the bottom line. It is easier for to envision a fresh face than an existing IBM person. Yet, anybody who would be willing and able to work hard to understand the IBM Watson way, would give me hope. Besides all of the internal IBM fireside chats on management, Watson, Jr. wrote two best selling *My life at IBM and Beyond* and *A Business and Its Beleifs: The Ideas that Helped Build IBM.*

About IBM Wild Ducks

IBM CEO Thomas Watson Jr. was well known for his perceptions about how to motivate his people. He especially liked a certain type of employee which he referred to as a wild duck. As a long time wild duck myself, I fit right into Watson's IBM. Here are some words right from the Chairman: "We are convinced that any business needs its wild ducks. And in IBM,
we try not to tame them."

Former IBM Chairman Thomas J. Watson, Jr., wrote that: "In IBM we frequently refer to our need for 'wild ducks.' The moral is drawn from a story by the Danish philosopher, Soren Kierkegaard who told of a man who fed the wild ducks flying south in great flocks each fall. After a while some of the ducks no longer bothered to fly south; they wintered in Denmark on what he fed them. In time they flew less and less. After three or four years they grew so lazy and fat that they found difficulty in flying at all. Kierkegaard drew his point: you can make wild ducks tame, but you can never make tame ducks wild again. One might also add that the duck who is tamed will never go anywhere any more.

IBM management post Watson spent way too much time taming its wild ducks into conformance. IBM will not be able to be #1 again if it uses tame ducks in the operational force or in management.

Fundamental change for IBM is to bring back the spirit of the wild duck. It was a major ingredient in IBM's tremendous accomplishments during the Watson years. Why IBM abandoned the philosophy and went to textbook management will be written about for ages to come. It sure did not help the long-term growth of IBM's business and it set the company up for one defeat after another. Just look at IBM's post-Watson record. Show me the excellence. Think!

Great jobs for dedicated employees

Systems Engineer (SE), my position with IBM for twenty-three eyars, was the ideal job for a person who liked technology; a person who liked people; a person who liked challenges; and a person who liked to solve problems. I cannot help being a problem solver. Even today, I have to watch myself in my home interactions when my wife is describing a problem which she is experiencing. Before she is finished talking, my brain is working on the solution.

Sometimes, such as in a marriage that is not good unless one is asked. As a Systems Engineer, however, I was always asked and I had all of IBM to help me make sure that I had the right answers. IBM was a great company and it can be a great company again.

Think of the deal that the original IBM gave its customers before my first day of work in 1969. IBM customers loved IBM. They were not kidding. IBM saved many an IT Director's butt when they went left instead of right.

My job as an IBM Senior Systems Engineer was to assure that my clients, IBM's customers were able to effectively use their midrange IBM computer systems. The type of systems I supported cost from $100,000 to $1,000,000 when purchased directly from Big Blue. The dollar range for large systems products was $500,000 to $10,000,000 or more. My small business customers decided whether I was doing the job and IBM polled them every year to see if I was. IBM believed in many forms of report cards to keep employees in line and for motivational peurpose.s

I handled from ten to fifty customers who required various amounts of guidance and "love," and hand-holding to make effective us of IBM's computer offerings. Everybody from the CEO to the IT Director to the programmers to the operators to the keypunchers loved it when a Systems Engineer, such as myself, was on site. There would be a number of different personnel with whom I would meet, each having their own need, and each expecting me to solve whatever it was that was bugging them. I made sure I did.

Sometimes I would call on IBM prospects with an IBM Marketing Representative (salesman). The salesman took the lead and as he explained the new features in an IBM offering to the client, and how the new account prospect could benefit, more often than once, the prospect would look at me and ask if the product could really do that or how much work it would be to pull something like that off.

We got lots of orders from small businesses that knew little about computing because the IBM SE had to make it work. if I said it would work, my manager made me work as long as necessary without additional compensation to make sure it worked. My job was satisfied custoemrs. I learned to be a good SE.

When an IBM Systems Engineer had the good fortune of being with a salesman who brought in a new order, the SE often was immediately assigned to the new account and became responsible for the system being delivered on time and doing what was promised. Almost every time, the IBM team assured successful on-time installations and implementations. Failure in IBM was not an option. IBM customers grew to love IBM because we did the job.

For many years after I first joined the company, IBM customers rented their machines on a monthly basis. But in the 1980's IBM changed its procurement model for customers to a purchase / lease basis. The Watsons would not have liked that and so already at the time I was beginning to see certain decisions from the top of IBM that never would have been permitted if a Watson were in charge.

In my dream I was thinking back about why I liked IBM and why I always wanted to do my best for IBM when I was an employee. When I got to observe the Utica Branch Office team, I found a ton of excellent co-workers. The guys on the ground were sharp. Uticans Bob Irish, Sue Cassidy, Barb Niekris, Ken Cloud, Ken Sayers, and of course my favorite techie, Nick De Salvo were unmatched inside or outside of IBM.

Great employees throughout the old IBM

I was at two Utica Branch meetings when end of year results were being discussed and management was giving out cash awards and trips and prizes. It was like a game show. It was like playing for a sports team. It was really exciting but everybody knew only the top guys got the honors. There were no grab-bags. There was no socialism. IBM paid for excellence and excellence only. Nobody I saw looked jealous. I looked to see who the top guy was, and as I recall in Utica, it was Nick De Salvo—two years in a row.

He may have received other recognition but he was awarded a Systems Engineering Symposium slot both years, and the plaudits for Nick were not made up. He was that good. It made me want to be that good. The way IBM treated accomplished employees created a contagion in the ranks to be like that guy.

IBM today is different. Self preservation is paramount within IBM. IBM mamagers destroyed the quest for excellence over the years. It must be reinfused. The IBM guys that I know today, who work for the current IBM, are thankful to get through their day without being fired. If IBM could bring that employee trust and magic back, the company would be well on its way to success. Once IBM becomes excellent and successful by habit, getting to # 1 will be a less arduous notion.

I had worked with Sue Cassidy, Barb Niekris and others and they were all very good. When they corrected my neophyte coding (programming) errors it took me a while to see my obvious mistakes. There were no slouches in IBM Utica. One or the other years, both of these ladies, who were sharp as tacks got a trip to the Symposium.

In preparing this work, I tried to find a reference to an IBM Systems Engineering Symposium on the Internet and drew a blank. No hits! I would have copied IBM's description into this document so you too would know the official spiel. Maybe they don't have them anymore. That would be a mistake as it was such an uplifting experience for employees.

Just last night at a local pizza joint, my friends Dennis Grimes, Gerry Rodski, and I were reflecting on IBM in the olden days. Dennis began his IBM career on June 9, 1969, one week after our King's College graduation. He had two weeks in the IBM "old world." My first day was June 23, 1969, which was the first day of IBM "new world." It was the day IBM announced unbundling. Customers were to get six months of mutually planned support until the end of 1969, at which time, they would have to pay for an IBM SE (Dennis and my positions) to step on their property.

IBM unbundling of software and services

Since unbundling was the most serious announcement IBM had ever made about how it would conduct business , let's review what it was exactly: On June 23, 1969, under pressure from pending antitrust litigation by various competitors and the U.S. Department of Justice, The IBM Corporation announced that it would unbundle much of its software and services, and would price and offer many types of software and services separate from its hardware. IBM introduced the distinction between system control programs and program products (software); the latter became a salable commodity. In fact, for the non-IBM part of the computer industry, many credit IBM's unbundling as having created a bona fide software business. From that day on, anybody could sell software packages. They were no longer free with the hardware.

Under the announcement:

1. Systems engineering work would be priced on an hourly basis, except for marketing and sales support activities.
2. Equipment maintenance (field engineering) would be priced on a monthly fee basis.
3. Education was priced on a per-student or per-course basis, except for marketing and sales classes.
4. Custom programming was initially to be priced on a cost-plus basis, with the future option to bid fixed-price contracts.
5. Seventeen language, utility, and application software products were announced on a monthly lease-pricing basis, which included telephone support, error correction, and some future enhancements.

Dennis said to Gerry that unbundling made it seem to IBM new SE employees like the IBM job we accepted no longer existed. Some IBM managers such as his boss, conducted business normally as unbundling had really upset IBM customers.

My manager in Utica was by the book and took it more seriously. He told all Systems Engineers that we could no longer leave the office unless we had a full day of billing already completed or we had proof that we were going to a customer site to work on a services contract.

The big problem for SEs of course with a new offering, is that there were no contracts so SES who were not going to schools, and who were not part of mutually planned custoemr support, sat around all day. In Utica, we were prohibited from visiting customers or systems prospects. By the time my 18 months of IBM education was pretty well completed, the company had relaxed unbundling for Systems Engineering Support so much that it was like doing business in the "old world."

Utica and Scranton

I was a home boy and as much as I liked my peers in Utica, I hoped one day to work closer to home. Then it happened. IBM really cared about its employees. I had the good fortune of being transferred to Scranton in 1971 as an Assistant Systems Engineer, my current position in Utica.

My new manager, Bob Fratarcangelo in Scranton was a good manager and he immediately gave me a lot of responsibility. Sink or swim but there was always anothr competent SE in the office to bail out any SE who got in over their heads. Even IBM had bad managers, but most were better than good. I was very glad to be out of Utica, because of managers like mine who took the book too seriously. He must not have read the IBM Watson playbook.

The folks in Scranton were pleased to have another employee in the SE ranks. My friend Goerge Mohanco had transferred from Utica in 1970. The comics in Scranton always wondered what the other half of the trade was. Scranton got Kelly and Mohanco and Utica got what? They got a lot of paughs out of that.

Within six months in Scranton, I was promoted to Associate SE, and in record time, I was a full SE, then Advisory SE, and though I worked for IBM in times near the end of my career with Big Blue when one had to be a suckup to be promoted to senior level, without ever being a suckup, I was promoted to Senior SE. Why? Because I had earned it.

I had learned from the old IBM that if you do your job better than most can, you will be recognized if you deserve it. It was a great feeling in IBM getting regular raises—some outstanding, getting many bonuses, getting promotions, and getting peer recognition. The new IBM needs to go back to these old traditions when skill v socialism dictated the office stars.

Before I came to IBM Scranton, I noticed how much my peers in Utica respected IBM. I noticed how great salesmen such as Dick "Bucky" Flint could make a zillion dollars a year even if he took on IBM management about sales matters or quota matters. IBM had a ton of good will in its employee attitude banks.

Flint and I worked well together in Utica. He knew that I worked hard for our mutual clients. Besides A. Barton Hepburn Hospital in year two of my Utica tenure, in year one working with Flint. Hardin Furniture was my favorite account. We got the business and we served the customer well.

I grew up as a human being and as a knowledgeable systems engineer in Utica because of great people like Bucky Flint, Bob Irish, Ken Cloud, Barbara Niekris, Hank Donaldson, Nick De Salvo, Bill Campola, and Carol Longo. Thank you all. I was lucky to have met you all and you helped me know what working for IBM was all about.

Out of Utica

Getting out of Utica was not easy. George Mohanco had been discharged from active Army duty about eight weeks after I did. I had met George when I was in my last week of Army Basic Training and he was in his reception week. At the time, I had one stripe on my arm. I have no idea how we got together as planned as there were no cell phones.

When I went to the Reception Center at Fort Jackson to meet George, I was just about finished boot camp. Mohanco had just arrived. The "no-stripers" such as Mohanco were saluting me as if I were an officer. I had one chevron. I bought George a couple beers and I assured him he would get through it all.

I had a standing transfer request in to Scranton before I had gone away for Army Basic Training. When I got out of Advanced Infantry Training as an MP, IBM in Scranton had no openings. When George got out, they had a slot and he accepted it. When Utica hired seven people the year I was hired, they had more than likely overestimated their needs and Scranton, which was doing so well at the time, had more than likely underestimated its needs.

A year later, I was done with Utica. I was ready to resign from IBM to get out of Utica, NY for a number of reasons. It was the IBM management. At 23 years of age, I took a shot and I interviewed for the IT Director's slot at Marywood University. Marywood was located in Dunmore, just outside of Scranton.

In my interview with Marywood, I was offered the job on the spot. Sr. Eva Connors was the Business Manager and we "hit it off," in the interview. I told my IBM boss that I was leaving IBM. I did not ask for a transfer it was already on my record. I really did not want to leave the company, just Utica. He said: "Give me a day!"

Transfer to Scranton, PA

The next day he told me I had an interview in Scranton and I can assure you I got to that interview on time and I got the job. My toughest assignment after that was to inform the trusting Sister Eva, who was a wonderful person who died well before her time, about IBM transferring me back home. I wanted the Marywood job very much. When I came to Scranton IBM, as luck would have it, I was assigned Marywood as my account. Sr. Eva warmly accepted me.

I learned when I came to Scranton that there had been a number of people, some of which I did not even know, who were pulling for me to get the transfer from Utica. IBM people were always the best. One of these folks was Tony

Opalski, my original IBM mentor, and another was a guy I had never met who went to the same college as I. His name is Al Teufel. I still thank him in my heart for his help.

Al had gone to Scranton Management and had spoken of me in the finest terms from information he had received from George Mohanco. Thanks Al, you are one of the reasons why IBM can again be the best. All IBM has to do is hire guys like you and Tony Opalski. What a lucky guy I was to know you both.

IBM Recognition -- Symposium

Eventually, I got to go to my very own first Systems Engineering Symposium. I learned why it was a quiet blood fight for SEs to do their best job in all circumstances so they would get the nod to go to this great event. Once I got to go, I never wanted to miss another and I racked up many symposiums until close to the end of my career when socialism took over in IBM and the biggest reason an SE was given a slot was because he or she had not been picked in a few years.

Some in IBM might suggest that a Systems Engineering Symposium honor was no big deal but they are wrong. It was the top yearly honor. When only the best were picked to attend, all members of the team wanted to be the best. IBM knew how to motivate people in those days. SE s who wanted their chance at a slot worked even harder the next year. They did not whine to management that they never got to go. I know I felt good about myself and wanted to work hard every day for the IBM Company. IBM can get that spirit back in its team if it chooses to do so.

I credit IBM for the great opportunity the company gave me in my life. During Systems Engineering Symposia, I got to hear speakers such as Buck Rogers, President of the IBM Data Processing Division and the best speaker in IBM. I got to hear other great IBM chieftains, often the CEOs, who were simply unavailable in the Branch Offices. I learned about IBM and about IBM's plans and how IBM thought about the economy in general. I learned business from businessmen. I got to see so many IBM executives, that if given the opportunity, I could have given all of them some good advice. That is what I am doing in this book.

In addition to the best speakers in IBM who most often held the top positions, IBM paid for the best motivational speakers that money could buy. I had the great pleasure of being motivated by the likes of Merlin Olson and Richie Ashburn. Moreover, the venues were the best such as LA, SF, LV, NO, Nashville, etc. What a treat! At these events, I can remember top flight entertainment in their prime such as The Beach Boys, Andy Gibb, Frankie Valli, Michael Iceberg and many others. Great recognition needs to be part of the new IBM to help keep a top level spirit in the troops.

Every now and then IBM would contract with a speaker whose name I would not remember but whose message was so good I could not forget it. Let me tell you one of these stories.

You have to care about your job

Comedian/ Motivational speaker X at an IBM Symposium told a story about a chicken and a pig. He was talking about not getting too frazzled trying to do your best for the company. Just go ahead and do your best and don't worry.

He cautioned the audience to always work hard but not so hard that it affects your ability to be a great employee. In his story he talked about a chicken and a pig and a great breakfast. He asked every person in the audience to imagine a great ham and egg breakfast—the best breakfast they had ever had.

Then he said now let's look at this great ham and egg breakfast in detail again as we discuss the pig and the chicken. He gets the punch line look on his face and he asks everybody to look again at this fine breakfast. He then says sometimes too much is too much. For example, in this ham and egg breakfast, the chicken is involved, but the pig is committed. You have to care, he said. But, not that much! Having part of your body on the pan frying was not a good idea for a committed work force.

Recognition was IBM

IBM made you feel like a million bucks most of the time, especially if you did something special. In 1972, I handled Sturdi-Wear Clothes in Taylor, PA, a division of USI. Al Teufel was the Marketing Rep. He was the best. I did all the work from design to implementation to specific function coding in order to put an IBM 2770 Terminal in South Carolina.

I helped the IT Director code the special parts of the program to dial South Carolina; receive the payroll cards from the South, process them, and then send the printout back. I did this with something called the RPG TP Feature. When it was all over, the 2770 printer in South Carolina that was loaded with blank payroll checks, printed out each check perfectly.

I thought it was just part of my job. Al Teufel thought it was something special. He spoke to IBM management about this achievement. IBM provided me the distinction of a $750 Regional Manager's award for the effort. At the time, it was close to 10% of my salary.

Chapter 2   This Dream Has a Basis in Reality!

IBM when motivated, makes dreams come true

This book as noted several times is about a dream I had. I now know that IBM can make this dream come true. It is a dream about IBM becoming # 1 again in the Information Technology Industry. Would IBM refuse an opportunity to be # 1 again? I think we are all about to find out.

I Had a Dream that IBM Could Be # 1 Again

Many are confused by IBM's failure to highlight its best products and its willingness to give up too soon on many other fine, innovative products that the company at various times would not promote.

The IBM I grew up with was part of an IBM that always could. There was no *can't* in T. J. Watson Jr.'s IBM. There was no group of IBMers that I ever met that were *No-Way-Jose* guys. All were as dedicated to the Watsonian spirit and the Rochester Lab in Minnesota, a part of IBM more like Watson than all other divisions was at the peak of its game.

Thomas Watson Jr. wanted IBM to be the best computer company in the world. His dad, T.J. Watson, Sr. wanted IBM to become the most successful business in the world. Both got their wisesh before they died.

IBM invented the mainframe computer under Tom Jr.'s watch and it was as elegant a design as could have been produced for 1964. Watson Jr. spent $4 billion of IBM's massive cash reserves on the project and he borrowed another $1 billion to make sure he had enough.

Watson had designed with his team the finest mainframe computer system that God had ever permitted to be designed. When it was ready to become a reality, it was built to succeed. It was called the System/360 representing the degrees in a circle. No matter what business you were in, a solution was available from the full circle of capabilities.

The idea was that no matter where a business was, the IBM System/360 could make their business run better. Over time, the mainframe contingent in IBM that Watson Jr. had created became full of themselves about their own merits and their value to IBM as a whole. Some say the mainframe division ran IBM.

When I began my career with IBM in 1969, I learned about unit record equipment (called TAB), the large electromechanical card processors from the 1930's that IBM was still selling to businesses across the world.

I got pretty good at wiring boards and actually wired an aged trial balance board from scratch. Techies who knew how to program should be in awe for what an IBM SE could do with wires, a circuit board, and an accounting machine.

Systems Replaced Electomechanical Beasts

Soon, while Watson Jr. was CEO, to reduce the expense of maintaining all the large electomechanical behemoths that were still making a profit while aging, IBM commissioned its electromechanical plant in Rochester Minnesota to build a less expensive machine to do the same functions that the large behemoths from the 1930's were still doing for the company.

And, so, in late summer 1969, after I had been to my first IBM schools and had learned how to wire boards for the huge units, IBM announced the System/3 as its machine to finally put the TAB equipment and the idea of board wiring to rest. Programming became the new buzz-word. Ironically, programmers call the act of programming, *coding*.

The System/3 was programmable in a new language called Report Program Generator II (RPG II) and it was built to be quite easy to use. It was an enhanced business language modeled after the RPG that had been introduced with the IBM System/360.

The System/3 had one flaw according to mainframe IBM. It was in fact a computer. Therefore mainframe IBM, wanting just large computers to survive in the company, prohibited the processor in this small business machine to ever grow to become a threat to mainframe opportunities with IBM's largest customers.

Even today, nobody challenges IBM in its #1 ability to make the most powerful totally packaged systems in the world. Yes, they are still referred to as mainframes.

Over time, the demand from IBM's small business customers to beef up the processor in the IBM System/3 and to create even smaller and less expensive units was heard by corporate IBM. The corporation smelled revenue. Nobody expected that the mainframe folks would be against this, but when these little machines became more powerful, things changed.

IBM kept the speed of the System/3 the same while helping it get more work done over ten years by adding faster disk controllers and fast Winchester hard drives and larger capacity disks. Then, when the System/3 ran out of processor gas with no place to go, IBM felt compelled to give something to the loyal customers who had invested millions in the product line while expecting their use of the system to be a long-term success.

IBM saw many millions of dollars on the table if it could simply satisfy the needs of the small customers whose computing requirements had grown. Of course Big Blue had to be able to accomplish this without compromising IBM's cash desire from mainframe sales.

Looking ahead, IBM's Lab in Rochester, Minnesota where the System/3 was built and its OS was created, hired the necessary people and put forth a new endeavor to assure that IBM could continue bringing in cash from its smaller systems. The effort resulted in the largest project the little IBM Lab in Rochester ever took on.

Labeled the Silverlake Project internally, the mission was to create the S/3 follow-on product. The design had been done already by an IBM group commissioned to create IBM's mainframe future system. The project used the Future System FS elements put for the by IBM's most brilliant computer scientists to create the specs for its follow-on to System/3 which was named the System/38.

IBM itself chose to enhance its Sytem/370 machines in an evolutionary style rather than create a revolution in its largest accounts by ofrcing them to swith to the totally different Future System (FS).

The System/38 used techniques that even mainframes could not implement and it was so sophisticated that its time frame for development was extended by more than a year as the tasks were so great. In other words IBM could not deliver the system when promised. IBM took people from all over the world to bring the System/38 and all of its sophistication to the world as soon as possible.

I was asked to put in an obligatory two-week stint while the System/38 product was moving from test to production. I never thought it would ever make it as a mainstream, clean IBM product as it was crashing all the time. Yet it did. It was much more stable on my last day in Rochester than my first.

In November, 1980, IBM in Scranton. PA installed three of these new systems. I was the System/38 coordinator at the time and so I worked with all three new System/38 installations. It was my job to make sure all were very successful. After an announcement in June 1978, it took almost 30 months for the first System/38 to be instlaled in Scranton, PA. It turned out to be worth the wait. It was the most advanced system ever built. No system today from Intel or Microsoft or even IBM's mainframes compare with the architectural sophiscication of the 1978 System/38.

The System/38 was very successful and it ran clean. It was a programmer's dream. After a successful run, IBM's Lab in Rochester got permission from corporate IBM for the follow-on to the System/38 with a project known as Olympic. The mainframe division was not happy about this as the power of the system would reach that of the smaller IBM mainframe systems and IBM mainframe personnel cautioned Mother IBM that the company should not want to eat its children.

I hate that phrase. Don't you? They would have squashed the System/38 follow-on if they could have. The IBM company had no answer to the minicomputer revolution and IBM's small mainframes were getting beaten badly in the marketplace by all of the minicomputer vendors of the day. These included DEC, DG, Prime, Wang, and HP.

The long-anticipated Application System / 400 (AS/400) was announced in June, 1988 and it was an immediate success. IBM could ship units almost as soon as it had announced their availability. Within a few years, the minicomputer competition including the vaunted DEC were finished. IBM had put them to bed for good. Corporate IBM had used what it saw as its ugly stepchild (the AS/400) to save the corporation from embearrasment. The minicomputer threat was gone.

Those pundits and industry watchers looked at the System/38 and the AS/400 and were amazed at its construction. Its architecture and its revolutionary computer science capabilities had not ever been seen on any computer system ever and still do not exist on any other modern day computer. No system on earth was as elegant or as powerful in its elegance as the IBM AS/400. The /400 was a much faster and more capable system than System/38. Itt was based on the same IBM FS characteristics as the IBM System/38.

IBM could have owned the IT world

There are many of us who worked for IBM at the time that believed that if IBM were not protecting the mainframe business, the company could have won all of the business data processing accounts that were ready for a new system. IBM's mainframe division kept the company from a winning strategy.

Some of us who were part of the System/38 and the AS/400 announcement period and subsequent implementations, are still convinced that IBM has never built a better system nor a more sophisticated, more capable, yet easy to use operating system. IBM could again be # 1 if it looked into its research labs, dusted off its best marketing material and went out and sold its best product ever. .

The AS/400 was built so that it could run System/ 32, System/34, System/36, and System/38 programs right out of the box. It was the finest machine based on futuristic specifications that any division in IBM had ever produced.

Looking at what is happening in IBM today with cloud computing and some other innocuous implementations, there is nothing supercalifragilisticexpialidocious coming from the IBM labs anytime soon. I am including of course even things whose sound may seem atrocious. IBM still has nothing exciting coming from the labs to make a user of any system think that Ah! Ah! IBM finally has the best answer.

In a subsequent edition of this book, I would be pleased to include a rebuttal from IBM about any of the facts, analyses, or conclusions that Big Blue may dispute. However, I think I am right. If IBM provides me incontrovertible evidence that I am wrong, I would be happy to add IBM's story to my own, in the Second Edition of this book to get a complete story. Remember this book is not about slamming IBM. It is about helping IBM become # 1 again. Undoing bad decsions of the past would be a good step # 3 in the plan to be #1. Adopting FS technology to win the war of the worlds of computing is the fourth and final step.

I am interested in IBM surviving and thriving. But, IBM must change its ways, develop a plan, plan its attack, and work its plan day-in and day-out. Over the years, IBM has broken some cardinal rules of marketing such as not paying attention to its customers and not protecting its assets. I have not treated IBM harshly in this book but I do believe IBM has treated its AS/400 customers and consultants very harshly—especially those that beg the corpration's marketing department to do something to increase sales.

I can appreciate that IBM would want the gloves kept on when it is the object of reproach for letting FS go into the dustbin while highlighting tired mainframe technology. Big Blue has not been fair to its customers.

While telling IBM how to succeed and become # 1 again, I have taken every opportunity in this book to show how and why IBM has been in a forty-five year slump. I am fair in this book, but I am definitely not balanced. The balanced part of this book will come from IBM's corrective action or perhaps its rebuttal. Among lots of other things, IBM has got to want to be #1 in order to make it back to the top spot.

At any rate, I hope that at the very least, along with learning a number of things, you enjoy reading this book. I sure have enjoyed writing it. IBM can again be #1 and I would be pleased to help.

There's more to come... Hold on!

Chapter 3   The IBM #1 Dream Includes Employee Trust

IBMers shoot for # 1

There was a lot of good stuff in my big dream that said IBM could be # 1 again. Nick De Salvo in IBM Utica thought IBM was # 1. Ken Sayers thought IBM was # 1. Dennis Grimes from Poughkeepsie thought IBM was # 1. Al Teufel in Marketing thought IBM was # 1. IBM was kind enough that it made all of its employees think that the Company really was #1 because of us. IBM was # 1. We were #1. IBM can be # 1 again.

Since IBM cannot fire everybody and hire a set of fresh bodies and then implement a new people-oriented Watson-like employee system, it must gain #1 with the horses that are in the barn plus some new ones. So, another key item for IBM is to regain trust with its employees and its customers.

No employee puts in 200% when they think they are a pawn in somebody else's story. Watson said that if IBM takes care of the employees the employees will take care of the business. That IBM has all but disappeared. The IBM employees outside the US are not taught the IBM Bsic Beleifs. What happened to that IBM? It can happen again? IBM can be #1 again but it cannot be #1 by acting like it has in the past.

Sam Palmisano took over at IBM about thirty years after Tom Watson Jr. retired from the job. Ginny Rometty took over after about ten years of Sam Palmisano. She is the current CEO. Sometime between Watson and Rometty, the trust disappeared with IBM, employees, and customers. IBM needs to win it back to be #1 again.

I don't want to suggest that the prior chair, Sam Palmisano or the current chair, Virginia Rometty were / are bad managers but today's IBM looks nothing like the Watson IBM, which existed when I joined the corporation. Maybe both are great managers. Maybe not! IBM must change to a company in which excellence is demanded in all aspects of the business.

I am not the only one who sees IBM squeaking by today rather than knocking the marketplace dead. There are many voices such as mine and Timothy Prickett Morgan's and Dennis Grimes' telling IBM to change the course and create some big thunder right away in the right way. Let the new IBM begin by reestablishing trust.

None of us, who are asking IBM to change direction are looking for an IBM safe approach in which the escape clause is a better option for the CEO than the success clause. A new IBM can emerge if IBM permits it. This new IBM must be much better than the current IBM if Big Blue chooses to go for it. IBM must make a decision soon and quickly to create a plan if it is ever to be # 1 again. I can't wait until I see the leaves moving again. Just the thought of IBM returning excellence to the corporation and planning to be #1 would cause immediate applause and a soaring stock price. Samle ole results in same ole.

I ask the current chairperson of IBM, Virginia Rometty to please read this book for the good it brings. I hope that it can help you Madame Chair along with your team of professionals to better figure out how to redirect the IBM we all see every day into an IBM for the future.

Nobody likes a company that is happy in the doldrums. I want a CEO that will put IBM into the living rooms of living, breathing business executives and regular people who might one day be customers or future executives. There is power in the message. The message is in fact far more important than the challenge du jour. I want every human being who sees IBM's message to want to be part of the Company's success even if they do not know why IBM is so good. I want IBM to tell people about its hidden secrets. Why are IBM's untold secrets so special? IBM's technology will knock the socks off anybody listening honestly to the message. I want people in their living rooms to fall in love with IBM. I know that can happen with the right message.

Some Great People Want IBM to Succeed

People all over the world including a great pundit, Timothy Pricket Morgan tell you, Madame Rometty every day, that you should use your trump card and get IBM out of the pickle barrel and put Big Blue on top again. Chapter 5, I have a great message for Ms. Rometty from TPM. But, not yet!

How do we go from a great dream about Utica and Scranton and then to words from Timothy Prickett Morgan. Don't worry…We'll get there! Prickett Morgan and many others in this business would love to see a #1 IBM Company.

It is so difficult to tell anybody who was not there what a great company IBM was before it chose not to be the best company any more. Industry Analysts such as Timothy Prickett Morgan are on the positive side for IBM and IBM customers all the time. He has made it his job to try to convince IBM's new managers from the top to the bottom that the corporation has not been making the right moves. He is more subtle of course than I. He is a great writer and a great thinker and a great lover of IBM technology and the one-time IBM way!

Some IBM CEOs were misguided

In the 1980's in the John Opel days, IBM decided that as long as it could be the *low cost producer* and have a zillion plants, nobody would care if the company had forgotten about the

Watsons' beliefs. When John Akers took the helm, the IBM
ship was off course. Worse than that, it would veer left or
right regardless of Akers futile attempts to steer it straight.
Opel had taken the hidden treasures in the ship and had
pillaged them. He had taken some secret treasures and buried
them deeper so that Akers would not think to use them to
recover IBM from the dilemmas he inherited.

With huge positive earnings during Opel's time, Akers
thought his ten year tenure as CEO would be a cake-walk. He
had no clue what Opel had done to him and done to the rest
of IBM. He did not know how to rescue the old IBM from
the archives when Opel had destroyed IBM's future earnings
picture. Akers found himself and IBM on death's doorstep.
He needed cash and had no products that could give him
what he needed so he simply tried to sell the company one
division at a time. While I was with IBM it was as if every
division was for sale if the price were right. Akers hoped the
pundits and the board of directors would think this clever
way of raising cash was a great idea. They didn't.

More than anybody, Opel and Akers destroyed the old IBM
and forced the new CEOs to treat the company differently
just to survive. Somewhere between Opel and Akers there is a
villain and a victim.

It took Lou Gerstner who was euphemistically known as the
cookie man, from his career as CEO of Nabisco, to use the first
fully functional, unencumbered intellect in IBM since
Watson to solve the 1993 IBM dilemma. IBM was in the
process of being dissected by Akers to pay for Opel's debts
when Gerstner noticed that if he let it go, there would be no
part of IBM capable of creating products to sell.

Gerstner figured his IBM was better off with something
rather than nothing so he stopped the errant selling of IBM
assets and he settled the company into things that it could do
to make revenue that did not require a complete sell-off of the
company. Opel and Akers did not have a clue about what
IBM could do to save the company. Both were salesmen at

heart. It took the *cookie man*, who was a great businessman to save IBM from its former self.

Lou Gerstner used his own intellect.

Mr. Gerstner chose to concentrate on Software and Services to save IBM. His job was not to make IBM the best in anything. It was to save IBM from destruction. When things calmed down. Mr. Gerstner had already had enough and he retired from IBM as a big success. He saved Big Blue from itself.

When he left, I feel he did none of us IBM lovers a favor when he more or less appointed a career IBMer, Sam Palmisano as the CEO. All inbred IBM CEOs other than Learson after Watson Jr. had failed IBM, its customers, and its employees.

Post Gerstner IBM groping for Revenue

From what the business pundits suggest, Sam Palmisano used financial gimmicks to prop up earnings. At his exodus, he more or less appointed Virginia Rometty to head the vaunted IBM Corporation as CEO and Chair from then 'til now. Meanwhile from that point, revenue has been heading south, with no really good explanations.

I do not know either Palmisano or Rometty but neither seem to be adventurous enough to try to figure out what products might have been in the IBM storehouse or in the design lab that might have become or still may become springboards for the Company's future success.

There are a number of innocuous terms being thrown about but the biggest one today is cloud computing. IBM has a habit of announcing a notion and then removing all vestiges of the prior method. Cloud Computing is a very complex idea that is based mostly on premise than on reality. It can make it big but then again; maybe it won't. I would not bet the farm on it. IBM is not the only player in that game.

IBM has spent billions of dollars building its cloud business globally with a number of acquisitions in 2015 that include Clear Leap, Merge Healthcare Inc., Gravitant, Inc., StrongLoop, Inc., Blue Box Group, Inc., Explorys, etc. I personally think Cloud is a good idea just like service bureaus have always been a good idea, but IBM will not be #1 with Cloud alone. Many top competitors such as HP are looking at Cloud and will work to stop IBM from becoming King of the Clouds. Here are the major players today in Cloud Computing (alphabetical order):

- Amazon
- Google
- HP
- IBM
- Microsoft
- JoyentCloud
- Rackspace
- Salesforce.com
- VMware

Amazon and Google are companies that seem to be able to do anything. Amazon for example works with Kindle and CreateSpace to provide an easy to use service offering to authors who write books. I have recently begun to use these services. I don't care in the Amazon cloud what the hardware or OS is. I just care that they can get my book edited, published, and printed in a painless way. IBM has no offering of which as a very small businessman, I can use. Consequently as an IT expert and as a businessman myself, I would not want the IBM stock price to have to depend on Cloud Computing and just Cloud Computing.

As a reader of a book that suggests IBM can be # 1 again, you must be wondering what I think about all this. Well, I have a lot of thoughts besides Cloud Computing which I gave above, and I have a lot of friends who have a lot of thoughts. All of us know that with IBM as our thought competition, our thoughts will remain impuned.

A celestial being observing from outer space would suggest that IBM stopped thinking about real success years ago. Its road to # 1 cannot be successful without somebody with power in IBM thinking differently. A *can-do*, rather than *can't do* attitude would help IBM as much as creating a trustworthy company. IBM must believe it can be successful and then it must take the actions necessary to become successful and then as quickly as possible go for #1.

IBM regaining its successful ways should be as easy as somebody inside or outside the company finding the key to the lost storage bin of great IBM thought and rescuing IBM's ability to think. My fear and yours of course is that the new IBM would object to such an inquiry, and would not invest any money or energy to find the key.

Maybe IBM does not deserve to be # 1?

If that is true then unfortunately, IBM cannot and will not make it to # 1 and in fact may fail completely as a company. But, I did not write this book so IBM would not make it. We stockholders must take action through the board to make sure IBM gets back on track. The board is elected and it must put the right leaders in place to win. The IBM future track must lead to #1.

Being in midrange systems from $100,000 to $1,000,000 purchase price for years, one of my biggest frustrations and the frustration of my peers also is that for all these years, IBM seemed like it was not even trying to be successful. Like the Emperor who found out his attire was only skin deep, IBM must put on a new set of clothes and must make all attempts to be successful. On its way to a successful future after its makeover, IBM needs to point itself to #1 and stay on target.

Chapter 4   IBM Once Planned Its Best Future

A Future System FS architecture must dominate IBM's future

As you will learn as you go through the chapters of this book, IBM had created the best computer architecture with the help of all of its laboratories. Nobody on earth had even conceived of what IBM had already implemented. IBM called the project Future System (FS). Big IBM said it would not permit this future project to become a system. IBM's best people said that the System/370 with just a few extensions were all IBM needed to lock-in its large systems future.

Yes, FS was supposed to be the next mainframe but Big Blue refused to give the OK to build a mainframe with FS characteristics. So, when IBM needed a replacement for the System/3, rather than choose an also-ran processor and architecture, IBM's bright Rochester, Minnesota Software laboratory dusted off the mainframe FS project architecture material and speced out a system that would be its embodiment but would run on a hardware processor that would be lots slower than mainframes.

Eventually, IBM announced a machine designed and built in Rochester, Minnesota that had taken the implementation team over seven years to create. It was announced as the IBM System/38 and as simple as that name sounds, this machine has yet to be surpassed architecturally by any commercial computer in existence today.

More importantly, though nobody refutes how great this machine actually is. All computer vendors today realize they do not have the capital and the wherewithal to create a machine like it. Adding the thirty-eight years of enhancements to the IBM System/38 and you have a system that only the old IBM would relegate to the back-burner.

The Future System (FS) is so complex internally that IBM, a company with more system development horsepower than any software or hardware computer lab in the world, had to delay its availability by two years after having announced it. It was so complex and so unique internally that even IBM could not make it work on time.

That put an awful lot of egg on Chairman Frank Cary's face and he did not want to risk a repeat. Cary brought people to Rochester from IBM locations all over the world to assure the viability of the Future System (FS) which would be announced as The System/38.

You might ask why this is relevant in a book about what IBM needs to do to be # 1 again. First of all, we must remember that the IBM FS project was not initiated by a small lab in Rochester Minnesota. It was commissioned by the top officers of the IBM Corporation.

Its purpose was to create a system that would be so advanced nobody other than IBM could afford to build it and it would last "forever." Moreover, customer application programs would never need to be changed. That of course was a tall order.

By the way, to this day, other than a research project here and there, no commercial vendor has ever created a machine as sophisticated and powerful. Even IBM's mainframes do not possess the characteristics of the advanced Future System, which, after the FS design was the product of a seven year effort by a team of engineers that did not have the word *NO* in their vocabulary.

Only IBM could have built FS. The fact that IBM built it in Rochester Minnesota without their greatest mainframe gurus is a testimony to the ability and hard work of "*A little lab that could!*" The fact that IBM at the corporate level would not acknowledge its company's greatest achievement since System/360 points to sub-par management.

That's why I wrote this book. It is never too late for the best to prevail. Greatness does not come around too often. IBM missed its chance but AS/400 aficionados and pundits such as Timothy Prickett Morgan believe in second chances. IBM, you got your second chance to be #1. Now, take it! Don't sit still!

Rehashing the FS Project

Let's take a minute to say this again in more specific and less colloquial terms. It helps to remember that in 1969 and 1970, shortly after the IBM System/370 was announced, an economic slowdown and then a recession affected the computer industry. There was big concern in IBM that the boom years were finished as IBM's mainframe revenue growth had all but vanished.

Technology was moving so quickly that there was fear that computers of all kinds would become cheap to build much too quickly for a company interested in sustained profits and growth from its hardware investments. At the time, Bill Gates was just a pup and nobody was making big money from software of any kind.

Predictions of dramatic price drops in transistorized memory and disk memory coming within the next ten years created fear in the board rooms of technology corporations across the world. Members of IBM's Corporate Technical Committee (CTC) were convinced that a completely new architecture was needed for the future. The consensus in IBM was that System/370 was not enough to sustain the future.

IBM knew the task would be large. Emerson Pugh quoted IBM in his groundbreaking book, *Building IBM* as saying: "This [FS] is a major undertaking and a task equal to, if not larger than, our change to System /360." IBM had spent $5 Billion bringing the S/360 to market in 1964. The last million for the System/360 was borrowed capital.

Tom Watson Jr. bet the IBM Corporation on the System/360. IBM hoped it did not have to do this again but it felt the handwriting was on the wall that such a move would become necessary in the short term. With the competition ready to devour IBM at its first opportunity, the corporate thinking was to get the project rolling much sooner than later.

To get this job done, great IBM people had to be reassigned to the effort. A major task force led by John Opel, was set up in August 1971. Opel was a rising star in IBM who went on to become IBM Chairman and CEO in 1981. The team reviewed several proposals before choosing George Radin's proposal for a single-level store, capability-based architecture. (Radin was well known at the time as a pioneer in the creation of the PL/I language.)

The devised architecture became known as FS (Future System) in IBM. It was to be the logical structure for the IBM mainframes of the future. System/370 would be the last of its kind was the hope in IBM's hallowed corridors.

IBM development typically never tries a new approach in just one way. Three implementations of the FS architecture were planned. The top-of-line model was being designed in Poughkeepsie, NY, where IBM's largest and fastest computers were built (water cooled mainframes). The middle model was being designed in Endicott, NY, which had responsibility for the mid-range computers (air cooled small mainframes). The third and smallest model FS was being designed in Rochester, MN, which had the responsibility for IBM's small business computers such as the System/3.

The best-laid schemes o' mice an 'men Gang aft agley. IBM's plans to whip up this FS plan in no time flat went astray. By the fall of 1974, the FS schedule had slipped several times, was well behind schedule. More importantly, IBM was enjoying record earnings under Frank Cary. The IBM S/370 systems were selling quite well.

Additionally, memory and disk prices had not fallen through the roof as predicted. And, so, Bob Evans stopped the rush and made a decision to extend the architecture of S/370, rather than abandon 370 for the future system design. Yes, Bob Evans gets credit for killing FS as a mainframe option.

By the way, Bob Evans was also known as Boe Evans. He was a well-known computer pioneer and corporate executive at IBM (International Business Machines). He led the groundbreaking development of compatible computers that changed the industry. His voice mattered.

The project was 100% killed in 1975. Not only did Boe Evans think it was not needed but the few cuts at implementation of the top level models showed exceptionally poor performance. IBM had so many "experts" on the project that it was marred by protracted internal arguments about various technical aspects.

In fact, one of the debates was about whether to use RISC or CISC designs. There was a contingent that wanted to do things with one hardware instruction to make software easier to build (CISC). This made the complexity of the FS prototype instruction set a major obstacle. IBM's own engineers felt the instruction set had become so comprehensive that it was actually "incomprehensible."

Bob Evans finally terminated FS when simulations showed that the execution of native FS instructions on the high-end machine were slower than the System/370 emulator on the same machine.

IBM Rochester was listening in

In addition to all other FS-interested parties, there was a Rochester group less than disinterested. To them it was not about the future of the mainframe. It was the future of the system that would compete against the mainframe if IBM were split up by the government. Moreover, they had a five year mission from 1969 on that charged them with planning for a replacement for the 1969-announced System/3.

They had begun their work before the System/3 announcement and they had met a number of times with the FS architects to see what it was all about. The "Rochester Team" was impressed with the design work of the FS group and they tuned in to many of the FS design concepts. They brought a lot of them home to Rochester for their conception of the System/3 replacement machine.

They worked on the new machine (FS-lite) for seven years. Their design work did not produce a lite version of anything. A mainframe team that had accomplished the FS Specs in iteration #1 as did the System/3 replacement team would have received a major IBM technical achievement award.

IBM announced what the watching IT world thought was its "mini FS" as the System/38 in October 1978 and delivered it finally in July 1980 after difficulties in implementation. It was a major technical accomplishment. It should have been heralded worldwide as the major technology accomplishment of the century but IBM would have had to explain why not the mainframe.

As many know, the System/38 later became known as AS/400, then the iSeries, and now it is known as the Power System with IBM I or as some folks like me call it, Power i.

And, so, although the FS project as a whole was killed, a *slightly simplified* version of the architecture continued to be developed in Rochester for the smallest of the three machines. The key term here is *slightly simplified*.

The finally released System/38 held true to most of the fundamental FS principles including single level store and capability based addressing. For this book none of this means anything other than that they were phenomenal computer science notions that had never been implemented on a commercial machine—ever!

A partial list of the never before implemented functions which were introduced with the IBM System/38 in 1978 is included below:

- 48-bit CISC-based architecture – IBM's largest hardware addressability at the time. Today, AS/400 is 64-bit
- 128-bit software architecture.
- Spooling and job management for multiple users/separate queues.
- Performance management for allocating resources.
- Single level store (S/38 unique).
- Technology-independent machine interface (S/38 unique).
- Integrated Relational Database (S/38 unique).
- Capability-based addressing for integrated security (S/38 unique).
- Object based (S/38 unique)

The only problem with the actually implemented FS machine (1978 System/38) if it were ever to be a major mainframe replacement was that it was 100% unlike the mainframe in its behavior. Another major obstacle other than no mainframe compatibility was that the mainframe division insisted that the new FS system's processor had to be a poor performer.

IBM at its corporate level did not want a mid-range computer system from Rochester Minnesota, out-performing a water-cooled mainframe from Poughkeepsie, NY regardless of how elegant or futuristic its architecture might be.

The system development team in Rochester had other goals that were more intrinsic and more far reaching than the S/370 team. The System/38 fulfilled those goals in that it proved to be a good architecture for ease of programming. Its only real issue was that it used an underpowered processor so that it would not be a threat to the mainframe S/370 team.

When IBM built the AS/400 in 1988 as the follow-on product to the System/38 it inherited the same architecture, but with major but not mainframe style processor performance improvements.

Ironically, the current version of the AS/400 (Power i) runs as a purely software implementation on top of the same Power chip that evolved from John Cocke's RISC machine.

Originally, there was a difference between the CPU used for IBM's Unix systems (which run the AIX or Linux operating systems) and the CPU used for the AS/400. It was one bit per 64-bit word to flag memory locations that contain the special addresses. Linux and AIX did not need single level store etc. In subsequent Power chip implementation, this difference was removed.

So, IBM's Future System lives on in the System/38 and the AS/400 and their successors, which I like to shorten to Power i. These Rochester inventions inherited almost all of the FS architecture—much more than the mainframe division would ever want IBM customers to believe.

Additionally, bits and pieces of Future Systems technology were incorporated in other parts of IBM's product line when appropriate but nothing compares to the all-out seven-year development of the System/38, followed by AS/400 machines and now Power I technology. The FS system has been designed, developed and implemented yet IBM keeps it a secret. It is today's Power i.

Power i will give IBM a winning chance

Part of IBM being successful in the future is to take the gloves off and fight inferior technology with superior technology. That ought to be a fair fight as IBM would surely win but only if it puts up its bester fighting machine and OS now known a Power i. Why IBM won't call itself the best is a conundrum for me. Cloud Schmoud! How about having a living implementation of a future system that can be sold and used commercially?

Yes, I am saying that after 1978, the vaunted cash-cow mainframe was no longer the most advanced system in IBM. That system was by all accounts at an architectural level, the System/38. Because IBM did not want its System/370 customers to demand that IBM beef up the System/38 for their scale of computing, IBM always low-keyed the power and capabilities of its finest computer system.

If IBM ever wants to become the #1 technology company again, in addition to changing its relationship with employees and customers to be more Watsonesque, it must make the AS/400 heritage systems pervasive. IBM can out-Intel Intel and out-Windows- Windows with the best hardware (Power) and the best operating system (IBM i) ever known to mankind.

IBM invested seven years making the AS/400 (System/38) work and it added 38 years of enhancements. This same architecture can run on PC-priced units and mainframe priced units. IBM can move its revenue from an almost $100 million dollar company to $500 million in ten years if it chooses to highlight its own FS technology as implemented in the IBM Power Systems of today.

Why doesn't anybody know about this? If you find the IBM manager that made this decision, please let us all know so we can through a stockholder resolution request that the Board fire that person.

Chapter 5   Corporate IBM Did Not Adopt FS—Why?

IBM liked mainframes the best!

Let me take another crack at this because it is so important for IBM's long term ability to be # 1 again. The reason IBM is in its revenue pickle today is that even when it had the technology in existing products that worked well, because of corporate parochialism, Big Blue would not acknowledge the superior architecture of its own System/38.

IBM corporate management stopped taking risks when T.J. Watson, Jr. stepped down. The IBM Execs feared that its mainframe customers would demand a similar system. For years, IBM downplayed its System/38 but when minicomputers began to steal the mainframe business, IBM decided that it would release the System/38 governors to kill the minicomputer competition.

In 1988, the System /38 was reincarnated as the AS/400 with lots more power, though the rationale supposedly was to enable IBM to destroy DEC and all the other pesky minicomputer manufacturers out there. IBM accomplished its mission v DEC and then more or less chose to mothball the AS/400 much to the chagrin of its AS/400 customer set. There were IBM customers out there that thought IBM would fully support the AS/400 and not try to turn it into something that the DEC people liked.

So how does IBM get back to #1? In addition to IBM changing its ways back to an employee and customer friendly company, in this book, we suggest that IBM at a corporate level must take another good look at the AS/400, now known as Power i and adopt the platform across the spectrum from laptops to desktops to servers to big moose system.

IBM needs a top to bottom revamp of its systems and operating system strategy. Why not pick the best IBM system ever developed to be its champion at the hardware level and at the OS level. IBM is the best at both, hands down. Why should Big Blue not present itself as the best?

Additionally, there needs to be a renaming of the poorly titled RPG programming language so that the world knows again that IBM is back in business and this advanced language is the backbone of its future success. IBM mainframe customers will buy mainframes for ten years after they learn that the System/38 had a better architecture than any mainframe has today. Forget about an alpha test or a beta test for IBM's new mainframe, the mainframe future architecture, first implemented in 1978 with System/38, now known as Power i. is ready to be implemented with IBM's fastest Power 8 processors.

IBM can get lots of help in coming up with advertising copy material so the world knows that it is serious about having the best #1 technology this time. The next formal event in ten years will be that IBM is crowned # 1 computer company in the world.

Just the other day, my good friend Paul Harkins (http://www.harkinsaudit.com), who also thinks that IBM can do better with its pace-setting technology, sent me a copy of Timothy Prickett Morgan's AS/400 28th birthday message in case I had not seen it.

I have not been discussing my dream about this book and about IBM being on top of the pack again but judging from his piece, Prickett Morgan has been tapping into my dreams. Or perhaps it is vice versa. Either way, I love his work in this regard.

One of the greatest advocates for the AS/400 platform is Timothy Prickett Morgan http://www.itjungle.com/biotpm.html. This is one of Mr. Prickett Morgan's best messages to IBM and to the AS/400 following for all to see. He is telling us all something—especially IBM.

The AS/400 At 28: A HENRY, Not A DINK

Published: June 20, 2016   http://www.itjungle.com/tfh/tfh062016-story01.html
by Timothy Prickett Morgan

A lot of people get credit for the work that went into creating IBM midrange systems over the decades, and rightfully so since the creation of such machinery, including the hardware and the software, takes many hundreds or thousands of individuals with each successive generation. It is appropriate to think about them as the AS/400, the forebear of the current Power Systems IBM i system, turns 28.

That is a long time in a human life, and an even longer time in computer history, where a generation has spanned from 12 to 24 months instead of decades. The funny bit is that the span of a computing generation is stretching out to maybe more like 30 months these days as Moore's Law slows, and the younger generation is also stretching the time between when they are born and they bring the next generation into the world.

It is not at all unusual for kids these days to be 30 to 35 years old before they settle down and grow up. (Funny juxtaposition of phrases there.) In fact, I have heard a new abbreviation for this generation: HENRY, short for *High Earners, No Responsibilities Yet*. The *yet* is the key there, and it is what separates these people from DINKs, which means*Double Income. No Kids* and implies that this will be the way it is for these particular couples.

The generations stretch over time, and we have to go back from time to time to learn--and often relearn--what others did.

Each year, as the AS/400's June 21, 1988, birthday rolls around, I get to thinking about the evolution of computing and how strange it is that this machine exists at all, what a success it has been in terms of innovation and market acceptance over the years, and also how its predecessors and follow-ons have come to embody a certain way of thinking that is both elegant and clever (as if you could have one without the other), and that equally importantly still brings value to the 125,000 or so businesses that employ it as the main system.

As I write this, we are also approaching Father's Day, so it is also hard not to think about the systems that led to the AS/400, significantly the System/3 from 1969 and the System/38 from 1978.

While Frank Soltis, the long-time chief architect of the AS/400 system and one of the key designers of the System/38, often gets a lot of credit for its development, he was one of many who fought for the machine and helped keep it alive.

One of my favorite people in the IT industry, Glenn Henry, who created clone X86 processors after leaving IBM in the 1990s with a company called Centaur Technology because he thought Intel's processor prices were too high, was instrumental in the development of the System/38 as well. I wanted to give him a shout out as well as to the good Doctor Frank.

If you want to read a fascinating interview, check out Henry's interview from 2001 that is part of an oral history of the computer business put together by the National Science Foundation and housed at the University of Michigan. This is how Henry responded when asked

about the thing that made him most proud in his
illustrious career:

> *"The thing I've done that I am most proud of is the System 38*
> *and I've done lots of things since then, but this is a very*
> *innovative system done by a bunch of young kids in the*
> *cornfields of Rochester, which was a backwater of IBM, and*
> *the system's key concepts are modern today, the system has*
> *survived today. I am really proud of the team. I'm proud of*
> *what I did there. Yes, so it took seven years to develop it, I*
> *mean, but it represented at the time, in fact at one point I*
> *made a chart, you know typical ACM paper, the 10 great*
> *advances of computer science--I made a list--we had seven of*
> *those on our system.*
>
> *You know, tags, storage, single level storage, integrated*
> *database, you know those types of things. We had built these*
> *into a commercial system and made it work and delivered it to*
> *customers, right, with little help from anybody. Research*
> *didn't help us at all. In fact, I have a very bad relationship*
> *with IBM Research, and it started here.*
>
> *They didn't support us. You would think that they would have*
> *but they didn't. The forces of the mainframe people were*
> *constantly against us, constantly chirping, trying to kill us*
> *because we were an annoyance to them. You know IBM was*
> *very competitive. They owned MVS and 360's and we were*
> *building this thing. They just saw it as some SkunkWorks*
> *project that would perhaps interfere with their grand scheme of*
> *things."*

This cracks me up. As I said last year around this time,
what does an in-memory database mean in a world that
doesn't have single-level storage? It means precisely that:
Your machine's architecture was so short-sighted that it
didn't have single level storage at all! The idea of
asymmetric processing is also coming back, we just called
it accelerated computing now. But it is still the same idea:
Offload certain functions from the CPU to intelligent

controllers lashed to the main memory of the CPU, and make it all look like a single collective as far as applications are concerned.

We are glad that Soltis, Glenn, and so many others fought the battles inside of IBM that allowed the System/38 to come into being and kept pushing so that a decade later the AS/400 made the System/38's core technology inexpensive enough that IBM could offer integrated relational database processing at the price of a System/36 that only had flat file databases. We just wish that the Power Systems-IBM i combination today was extended from systems of record to systems of engagement, the ones where advanced data analytics (which is driving an increasing part of the workload in the data center) is done.

IBM has to figure out a way to move Spark, Hadoop, and other workloads on to the IBM i platform itself, much as it has done with its System z mainframes, so they can run applications created for Spark and Hadoop even though these are very different from the architecture of the single-node, multicore Power Systems iron that most customers have.

I am not sure how to do this, but the machine can be partitioned and the complexity of the virtual cluster masked from end users. IBM needs to make sophisticated analytics that merges structured and unstructured data as invisible in 2016 as it made the relational database with the System/38 and perfected with the AS/400.

I know that IBM has no stomach for such things any more, but what I really want the company to do now that it has fully committed to the Power processor and platforms that are based on it is to create a next-generation AS/400 that takes the ideas of the system and applies them to modern, scale-out architectures while preserving (as much as possible) the single-level storage and asymmetric processing genius of the AS/400.

I suppose to a certain way of thinking of it, a Power9 chip with NVLink and CAPI ports talking to GPUs and other kinds of accelerators looks a bit like an AS/400 CISC processor with a few dozen or hundred Motorola 68K I/O processors hanging off of it to offload various kinds of processing from the CPU. The virtual and unified memory features that are going to be used in supercomputers based on Power9 chips and Nvidia Tesla GPU coprocessors are a kind of single level storage, we suppose.

We would just like to see a world where IBM i is a part of this, or that IBM would make Linux more like IBM i and therefore be able to run RPG, COBOL, Java, and PHP applications on the same iron that does simulation or analytics jobs.

In short, we want another generational change, one that embodies all the best ideas of today and that takes the IBM i [AS/400] platform into new realms and into the next decade or two. We have no idea what kind of software investment this might take, of course, or if customers would go for it. But we need a new Future Systems effort from IBM and its OpenPower partners that includes IBM i rather than just shunning it.

This is a lot to ask in 2016, we realize. But it sure would be fun to show that Google doesn't invent everything these days, and that you can, in fact, create a single platform that is good as a system of record and a system of engagement. That is, in fact, an Application System. Period. And that shows it was stupid to divide them up in the first place.

--- Thank you Tim----

Chapter 6   FS: Still unloved at 30 years old.

In 2008 Things Changed

In 2008, IBM revamped the AS/400 line again. This time it renamed what had been called the eServer iSeries to the IBM Power System (Hardware) with IBM i (Operating System). All the pasrt swere thre but now you had to buy te OS and the machine separately. Integrated is hard to sell when you need to buy two things.

I was distraught at the time. I had just finished a book titled, Can the AS/400 Survive IBM? And for me it looked like it had not. No one item such as the iSeries or IBM i5 or any of the other new names for AS/400 were relevant anymore since they referred to an integrated hardware and software combo. Now the machine and the OS were separate. So, I penned this article and sent it off to IT Jungle, and the respectfully printed it. In the article I went through the lineage of the product line so there is a lot here but it is accurate and often a source for the work of others on the Internet.

It is still available at
http://www.itjungle.com/tfh/tfh040708-story05.html

Goodbye, AS/400, Old Friend
Published: April 7, 2008
by Brian Kelly

The AS/400 is dead. Long live the AS/400. This phrase as associated with my favorite "midrange system" has changed over the years to meet the many successor systems that IBM has put forth to replace our good ole AS/400. In fact, even before the litany of replacement systems, the AS/400 itself was involved in a replacement act of its own when it was brought forth to succeed both the System/38 and the System/36. As we in this "AS/400 community" well know, nothing was and nothing will ever be as revolutionary to the world of computing as the System/38 in its day, even if we choose to call it an AS/400 or something else.

The System i, also known as our beloved AS/400, today is nothing more than an operating system. IBM would like us to see the new physical incarnation of the AS/400 in its new IBM Power System line. But, it isn't there. The System p has been able to run the i5/OS operating system for quite some time. It still can, but now with no holds barred. There is no new System i. IBM this week chose to remove the identity of the AS/400. It no longer exists under any name. Get used to it. Our old friend is gone. Besides AIX and Linux, these new Power 520, 550, and 570 servers also run a proprietary operating system known as IBM i. This fact enables it to run your workloads, almost as if your workloads are being re-hosted on a non-AS/400. Well, at least emotionally.

All of this is unsettling for me and for those of us who think a combination of box and identity removal is not the best way to highlight our favorite machine. Overall, it is a good time for IBM since its 25-year homogenization goal is all but accomplished. While I continue to digest the implications of last week's news, I thought I would sit down and put together a little piece of documentation about the good friend I remember so well. Goodbye, AS/400, old friend.

Now, don't say anything or I'll get emotional.

The Place Where Great Ideas Once Were Permitted to Grow
The IBM Plant in Rochester, Minnesota, first opened its
doors in 1956 and shipped its first product, the IBM 077
numeric collator. By 1957, the plant began pounding out
other mechanical units, such as the IBM 514 reproducing
punch and the IBM 523 gang summary punch. You see, in
the 1950s, there were no Rochester Labs creating the most
sophisticated operating system software in the world.
There was the beginnings of a plant complex that was
designed to build these huge electromechanical units, each
of which existed on a diet of lots more than 100 boxes of
80-column punch cards every day.

Even before 1960, this plant from nowhere established its
own engineering department and soon IBM announced
that Rochester was designing and developing its own
products. In 1957, the first two Rochester-designed and
developed units, the IBM 085 and 087 collators, were
shipped from a plant less than a year old. These units were
famous for such innovative concepts as *match*, *merge*, and
the infamous *match/merge*. IBM in Rochester was well on
its way to fulfill its legacy.

From the early part of the 20th century, IBM customers
were using expensive tabulating machines, sorters,
reproducers, interpreters, and accounting machines in
much the same way that the early computers of the 1950s
were used.

n the mid-1960s, computers such as the IBM 1401 and the
then-new System/360 were making major inroads in
larger companies across the world. Because IBM believed
there was still life in the notion of a "tabulating system,"
the company gave Rochester the mission of building a
smaller version of these punched card processing units
with some even less expensive report writing capabilities.
The exciting part was that Rochester was to do this from
scratch. The objective was to provide a simple solution for
the small business marketplace.

IBM's major computer facilities were located in Endicott and Poughkeepsie, two cities in New York, so this new, yet to be designed, small business-oriented miniature mechanical marvel was to be all done in Rochester. Considering that Rochester was blessed with the electrical and mechanical engineering know-how that could make the project a success, it was a natural fit. Please note that this to-be-designed unit was not supposed to be a computer

IBM 085 Collator Circa 1957

system, since IBM already had these two well-oiled plants that handled this mission for the corporation.

In the mid-1960s, in addition to the mechanical engineering teams, there were also computer scientists and computer engineers on staff in Rochester, since the engineering lab and the plant also built the card readers (1622 and 2501) and card punches (1442) for the IBM 1401 and IBM 1620, as well as the unit record gear for the System/360. Overall, Rochester made over 70 products at this time, each with major electromechanical components. There were always moving parts. With this mixed bag of mechanical and electronic experts, Rochester, as prescribed by Mother IBM, created the specifications for the smaller and less expensive next generation unit record system.

Rather than make the machine family all electromechanical, which would necessitate lots of mechanical parts, largeness, heaviness, bulky wiring panels, and cost, the engineers decided to build their "electromechanical" system using fewer moving parts by adopting the computer technologies of the day. Rather than use wiring boards to trigger actual relays, for example, as in the mechanical unit-record machines, the new unit-record punch card system would use small "computer" programs. To enable work to be accomplished, the "system" would be shipped with a means of translating source instructions in punched cards into programs. These programs would emulate the functions of the wiring boards of the past.

IBM 402 Accounting Machine Wiring Board
(Wire input to output)

The translating device of course would be software--a card-based compiler, very similar to that designed for the System/360 Model 20. This compiler language was not a new idea and had been, in fact, developed to provide accounting machine functions on IBM's 1400 series computer systems.

It produced programs with a fixed logic cycle that emulated the functions of IBM's best unit-record accounting machines (402, 403, 407, etc.). The IBM 1401 compiler was named RPG, short for Report Program Generator, since that was its function--to produce reports. When introduced for the new announcement in July 1969 (shortly after I joined IBM as a Systems Engineer), this compiler had been substantially enhanced and its new name was RPG II.

The chicanery of the Rochester team began with their full awareness that their mission was not to build a computer. They knew well that this mission rested elsewhere in IBM. So, no matter what, while this new machine was in development it was not called a computer, but rather a next-generation small business unit record system. The machine that flowed from this work would eventually be named the System/3. It would change IBM forever, offering ease-of-use IBM computing to small businesses for the very first time.

By the time it was ready for announcement, Rochester had named the machine, the System/3, which signified that, just as System/360, it was a computer system. Just as important as the word system in this scheme was the fact that the number was a single digit.

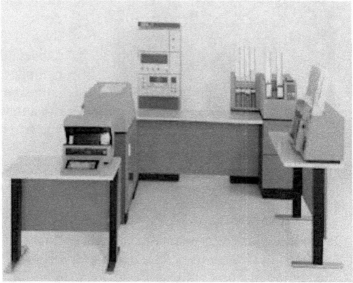

IBM System/3 Model 10 As Originally Announced July 30, 1969

This gave great solace to Endicott and Poughkeepsie as it helped assure them that IBM was not creating another mainframe plant that would compete with their products.

System/3 was simple, it was very capable and innovative. Pictures of the as-announced model and a later-model system, looked almost the same as the announced model. The original models had no disk drives, and card-based (unit-record) System/3 units were Rochester's only computer product for a while after announcement.

Note the vented drawers under the 96-column multi-function card unit (MFCU). These two optional drawers contained two 2.45 MB fixed disk units and also two 2.45 MB disk drives that used the flying-saucer-like disk drives scattered across the console table. That amounts to 9.8 MB of hard drive capacity on four drives. We've sure come a long way from such limited technology days, haven't we?

The notions of think small-sized and think inexpensive were prevalent as IBM Rochester designed the least expensive IBM computer at the time. It was, in fact, affordable by small businesses. The new 96-column card developed by Rochester was one-third the size of the 80-column punched cards and yet could store 20 percent more data. The industry was abuzz. IBM marketed the system well, and it sold quite well and gave Rochester a real place in IBM history and in IBM's future.

RPG for the Business System/3
The most significant innovation for IBM with System/3 was the perfection of the RPG programming language. RPG II for the System/3 was a real programming language. It was rich in business function and thus made the System/3 a real business computer. The language was instrumental in making the System/3 an instant success. It was simple. It was somewhat English-like, and it was not verbose or intimidating for new programmers, as COBOL was. Most of all, it was easy to learn.

IBM System/3 Disk System, card unit and printer circa 1971--One-Third the Size, 20 Percent More Data

Since there were not many for-hire programmers back then, the lucky folks tapped to learn RPG in the 1970s with System/3 were often young, bright, and trustworthy employees from blue-collar or white-collar departments. They held other positions in their companies and seemed like the right candidates.

Many of these programmers grew up to become the gray-haired AS/400 professionals who now, from their reserved perches on the world's finest cruise ships, still complain about IBM not marketing their favorite system.

IBM rewarded Rochester for its clandestine accomplishments by permitting the lab to continue improving these computers. The biggest and most powerful System/3 was introduced in 1973. It was known as the Model 15D. The unit-record façade for Rochester was officially over.

The IBM System/32 Is Introduced
With all of this innovation, the System/3 became a big hit in businesses all across the world, and Rochester became a big hit within IBM because it was making money for the corporation. In 1975, Rochester was at it again. The Rochester Lab introduced a System/3-like machine that was desk-sized. Notice I did not say desktop. Desk-sized was about as small as it got back then. This unit had a

keyboard and a small monitor, and had a printer attached to its back. It was an all-in-one computer called the System/32.

The System/32 used the same notion of Operation Control Language (OCL) as did the System/3 disk systems. The Set and the Key operations were taken from the System/3 Model 6 and made an integral part of System/32's interactive RPG.

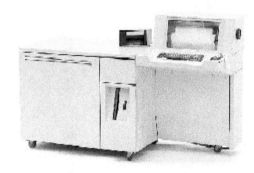

IBM System/32 Circa 1975

The system had one large fixed disk (up to 13.7 MB). As nice as it was, this desk-size box had one major disadvantage. It had just one input keyboard for interactive work. As such, the System/32 lasted just two years before IBM improved the design with a new and improved System/32. At the time, IBM was good at adding two to the model number as long as it did not reach three digits. So, this upgraded machine was introduced as the IBM System/34. It was constrained in size, but not in its tuning and device innovations. On its best day, total disk capacity was 27 MB.

After toying with terminal monitors on the System/3 such as the Communication Control Program (CCP), with the System/34, Rochester chose to make a terminal a real device to the operating system and to the RPG compilers. This brought ease of use workstation programming to the world. By also introducing the notion of multi-programming with the System/34, IBM enabled each user to have a piece of this one computer system as if it were

his or her own machine, and unlike mainframes, no
system programmer was required.

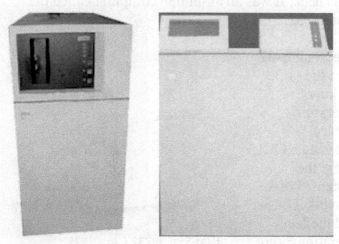

**The System/34 Multi-Station Computer and Its Follow-On,
The System/36**

The System/34 used terminals, but got around the
complexities of System/3 CCP.

Terminal management was built-into the S/34 System
Support Program (SSP) operating system. It was an
industry first. You could attach a number of semi-
intelligent, high-speed terminals to the system over a local
wiring type called twin-axial cable, without the need for
modems. The new terminal that IBM invented was big
and square, and it was called the IBM 5250. Each of these
terminals, at the time, could be purchased for about
$4,000. Though 5250s are no longer sold, the green-screen
5250 legacy continues today through PC products that
emulate the 5250 terminal's data stream.

The 5250 terminal had been built for Rochester's System/38 computer system, which was to be the follow-on computer to the entire System/3 line. In 1977, when the in-process System/38 was taking much longer to complete than originally anticipated,

A 5250 Terminal

Rochester decided to announce the System/34 and to use the terminals and printers that had been designed for the slowly developing System/38.

The System/38 Is Announced with Much Fanfare

IBM finally announced the long-awaited System/38, which had been code-named "Pacific," in October 1978. Rochester knew that the machine was not working well at the time, but somehow felt that it would be ready in 1979 in order to meet its planned first customer shipment. System/3 Model 15D customers, as well as many others, enamored by the outstanding specifications of the System/38, and the excitement of the System/38 marketing announcement, signed up in droves on the day it was announced for an early shipment of this new box.

Those who may recall 1978 and 1979 know that there would be no early shipments. In fact, there would be no shipments. In 1979, shortly before the system was supposed to ship, Frank Cary, IBM's chairman and chief executive officer, gave his humble apology and announced a delay of 11 months to make the system ready for business use.

If IBM actually knew how difficult it was going to be to bring out a system with the most advanced function ever available (including single level storage, the technology-independent machine interface, and the integrated relational database management system, the object file structure and tight compiler integration for all these components--all hallmarks of the AS/400) in even the largest computer systems, while still providing small system ease-of-use, I am convinced the project never would have been funded.

A monument to the practical limits of computer science, the System/38 finally arrived in 1980 to a mostly welcoming customer set. It was the best system that IBM had ever built with an architecture that is yet to be surpassed.

IBM's System/38, Announced in 1978

While IBM was bringing in the world of IBM to Rochester to work on the System /38 "problem," the System/34, with its 5250 workstations, caught on like gangbusters and shipped well over 100,000 units.

Fort Knox or Bust!
In the early 1980s, the mainframe division of IBM became increasingly alarmed that there were just too many IBM systems aimed at the same customer. Add to this the undisputed fact that IBM executives were never quite happy that Rochester built computers in the first place, and it was easy to see why things got a little dangerous to be employed in Rochester, Minnesota. IBM execs believed that real computers should be built in mainframe plants, such as Endicott or Poughkeepsie. It was tough to argue with success, however, as Rochester units were far more popular than their mainframe counterparts.

When you have a lot of money like IBM had, you can spend it on projects that go bust. So, the mainframe-oriented IBM Company spent hundreds of millions of dollars on a project known as Fort Knox to come up with one new system that would do everything that the System/3X machines could do as well as integrating functions from the Series 1 (basically, a glorified switch), and the smaller IBM mainframes of the day (the 43XX series). Since advanced chip technology was not one of IBM's areas of expertise in those days, the final design of Fort Knox was not one processor that could handle instructions for multiple systems.

Instead the hydra-like design was one processor in the system for each system that needed to be emulated. There was no notion of integration as with today's Power Systems. All the king's horses could not figure out how to put Fort Knox together, even one time. With processors being very expensive back then, this notion would never fly. It never got off the ground.

The System/36 was announced in 1983. It was an enhanced System/34 and offered more capacity and speed. By 1985, the Fort Knox systems convergence project, sponsored mostly by the mainframe plants, had gone bust.

The story many Rochester stalwarts were telling other IBMers at the time was that one of the secret goals of Fort Knox was to minimize the impact of the Rochester Lab on the company. The mainframe plants were a bit jealous of Rochester. [They still are!] Their idea was for the mainframe plants and labs to take over the Rochester systems work and send the workforce over to the Mayo Clinic for jobs. Of course, this also failed, but the disdain for Rochester and its products persisted in many important parts of the corporation.

Some might argue that the Power Systems convergence is a long-time-coming informal Fort Knox success, since the venerable System/38 and AS/400 names as well as the not so venerable i5, iSeries, and System i monikers have been cast off to the island of unwanted toys, along with the Ford Edsel.

Finally, the AS/400
For Tom Furey and other IBM Rochester Lab managers in the mid-1980s, life was not so good. IBM had taken all of the design dollars for the System/36 and System/38 follow-up systems and had given the dollars to the mainframe division, or to the Fort Knox project. There was no cash left for Rochester to create its follow-on products.

When Fort Knox went bust and the money began to come back to Rochester, the famous and infamous "Silverlake" project was launched. The Silverlake idea was to create one new hardware system that would replace both the System/38 and the System/36.

AS/400 B60--One of the largest AS/400 Systems

After little more than two years, in June 1988, IBM announced the results of Silverlake as the Application System/400, or AS/400. In many ways, the box was a repackaging of the System/38, with some left over Fort Knox parts, but it also ran System/36 programs untouched.

The original AS/400 was a resounding success by all measurements but one. System/36 customers were not too happy about it. They expressed their displeasure by keeping their old System/36 boxes as long as they could, and when they upgraded, they would buy either a second used System/36 (same size) or a bigger used System/36.

It took a long time for IBM's System/36 customers to warm up to the AS/400. However, there was enough new AS/400 business at the time from the former minicomputer vendors, such as DEC and Data General, that IBM did not have to care about not fully pleasing its own System/36 installed base.

Eventually, IBM was able to place the entire System/36 instruction set, as well as the AS/400 instruction set, on newer and better 64-bit RISC chips. With this change, the company was able to withdraw the Advanced System/36 from marketing several years ago. Today, the AS/400 can perform both System/36 and AS/400 operations.

AS/400 RISC Box Model 720 Circa 1999

In 1995, IBM introduced the AS/400 Models 400 and 500 series using the "Cobra" and "Muskie" PowerPC AS RISC chips. Users got to move to a 64-bit RISC architecture from a 48-bit CISC hardware architecture by merely off-loading and on-loading programs and data. The templates and abstraction facilities in the design of the System/38 permitted the CISC object code to move to RISC at 64-bits without a recompilation (because the operating system did the necessary recompilation in the highly virtualized microcode at the heart of OS/400).

Meanwhile, in the Microsoft world at the time, anybody going from Windows 3.11 to Windows 95 (from 16-bits to 32-bits) had to recode their applications--not just recompile. Re-code as you know is a code word for rewrite or write again that which was already written and working. How soon we forget. Too bad IBM could not sell its technical superiority while these major innovations were being released. But that is another topic for another day.

In October 2000, IBM recast the AS/400 as the iSeries and in 2004 the company again renamed it as the System i5 or just i5. This name ultimately morphed into System i. Until the launch of the Power 520 and 550 systems last week, most shops continued to call their OS/400 or i5/OS machine "the AS/400." I would suspect that the AS/400 will not die from our vocabulary until years after the last one has been shipped.

With all of the enhancements over its 20 years, the AS/400 has been the most architecturally elegant and capable machine in the industry. From the ground-up, it was built as an integrated machine. When you add this internal elegance to the Power6 engines that are now available with AS/400 technology running on them, the box was clearly the best and most powerful computer of all time.

The New Power-Based Power Systems
IBM has almost accomplished its Fort Knox dream of converging all platforms. Other than the mainframe, the job is done. From scads of different computers to just two computer lines today based on IBM technology: the mainframe and the Power Systems. I think we can expect that the mainframe will be joining the fold soon, and it is a fair guess to believe that X64 servers will also be brought into the fold. You can bet Fort Knox on that.

By the way, one might suggest that if you see the reduced revenue from hardware during the time period from which the Fort Knox project was scrapped until Power Systems emerged as its de facto incarnation, IBM bet Fort Knox that it could do it. IBM won that bet, but lost billions of dollars of hardware revenue over the years in so doing. Now, because of this death-wish desire to have just one computer line, IBM is about to have the revenue stream from just one computer line. Stockholders need to continue to thank former chairman, Lou Gerstner, for getting the software and services businesses going within Big Blue. That's where IBM is making its money today. Hardware, however, is becoming a diversion and so, the Power Systems will preserve IBM executive energy from having to deal with all of those different system brands.

In the short term, nothing will change for AS/400 shops--
especially if they opt to stay clear of V6R1 or the new
politically correct i 6.1. IBM enabled the Power6 chips to
be as integrated for AS/400 as the real AS/400 chips ever
were. Power6 just happens to also carry the water for the
System p and its virtualization and I/O processor
functions. Additionally, one can speculate that there are
probably some mainframe pretrails (as opposed to entrails)
on that little marvel of technology. So, if you go to a
Power System today, you will be better off tomorrow. It
has more, not less, and when supporting the AS/400's
newly named OS, i 6.1, it is as good, as and in fact better
than OS/400 or i5/OS V5R4.

What Is the Problem, Then?
So, what is the problem? Well, to me it's like General
Motor's Cadillac Division buying the Lincoln division
from Ford and announcing a convergence strategy on a
new luxury car called the Lincad. Nothing more is coming
for the Lincoln drivers who relish whatever the differences
are between the two. Nothing more is coming for Cadillac
drivers who also love to languish in the extra feature or
two that they see in their machine. Quite frankly, the
System i had an identity and has been neglected by Mother
IBM. Now, without a name or an identity, what should
we expect?

What is left for the AS/400 shop? Clearly, the notion of
real integration is passé with the new IBM. IBM now
makes its killing on software piece parts and erector set
services to put the parts together. There is no convergence
going on in Global Services or Software Group. They
make their money on your assembly pain, and the more
products you believe you need, the more pain there is.

The Web has been available for almost 20 years as a
commercial entity and it is the most important part of
many businesses today. Yet, IBM still treats it as a non-
essential (by which I mean a non-integrated) component.

It's handled on all platforms by the same piece parts software that works the same on all of IBM's platforms (and other platforms, too). Of course there are just two IBM platforms now. Piece parts development components and one size fits all rule the day. Depending on who you are, it can't get any better than that and likewise, depending on who you are, it can't get any worse.

Goodbye, AS/400, old friend. I'll miss you.

-- End of Brian Kelly IT Jungle article --

Chapter 7   More IBMers Must Be Visible to Customers

A return to a smaller sized Direct Field Force is needed to control the channels

When IBM was very successful, it had a field operation that was second to none. It was unbeatable. It included a direct sales force which included Marketing Representatives (Salesmen) and Systems Engineers (SEs). Systems Engineers would help IBM customers implement OS and application software and they would literally assure the customer's success by doing their best to solve problems and by marshalling any IBM resource that was needed.

For example, if bringing in the developer that wrote a particular line of code was needed to be brought to the customer site, in most cases we could get that done. IBM's support structure would have permitted us to get it done. I have been involved first hand. It was a big deal and that's why IBM was known for the best support possible.

There were also a lot of little deals that IBM provided that made customers happy that IBM was their vendor. These did not make the trade press annals. There were times, for example, that employees, sometimes from different IBM divisions, would shuttle needed parts from the repair parts plant to the customer location.

IBM person #1 would ride several hundred miles from the repair parts depot and hand off to # 2 etc. Eventually the customer got the repair part. This was simply to assure that the customer was up and running as soon as possible after a down situation. IBM did hand stands for customer satisfaction, I saw it firsthand. It worked and customers loved it and they loved IBM for it. IBM can be that company again.

Customers believed in their hearts that IBM would pay a zillion dollars if need be to assure its customers were happy. One of its basic beliefs besides respect for the individual was the finest customer service possible. When IBM dropped its midrange field force, its customers felt betrayed and very few new accounts came IBM's way after that. I

IBM changed its business model to distributor v direct sales and eliminated its Systems Engineering force and its direct sales force. IBM hardware and software sales tanked along with the specialness of the IBM—employee and the IBM—customer relationship. Something like this sprit needs to be brought back. Customers matter.

For IBM to make the comeback we are looking for, I am not suggesting reinstituting the very huge field force that the company once had. But, something between the employee numbers from then to now would be lots better than IBM customers never seeing IBM ever at all. Not seeing IBM is as good a reason as any for buying non-IBM. And, by the way, my close-up look at IBM Business Partners (ISVs) tells me that they do not have IBM's best interests at heart. That means they do not have IBM stockholders or employees' interests at heart.

IBM needs to know that and understand that and take control of its marketing channels. I know that IBM ISVS would turn leads over to Microsoft if a customer complained about a minor price difference. ISVs from my perspective had no IBM loyalty. An IBM salesman or manager who was assigned to the territory not to make the ISV happy but to make IBM happy could work—if IBM were serious.

Chapter 8   Back to IBM's Founding Principles

You Got to Dance with Them What Brung You!

Until the John Opel years, IBM practiced Thomas Watson Jr.'s beliefs about how employees and customers should be treated. Both Watsons had the right idea: "Take care of the people and the people will take care of the business." The Watsons cared about their employees and treated everybody fairly. IBM employees would always go the extra mile for IBM and IBM customers.

At my level in the organization, it took at least ten years after Tom Watson Jr. Stepped down that employees started to notice a difference. Learson was OK and Cary did not institute anything much different. There were no great ideas from Cary as would have come from Watson Opel and Akers literally destroyed IBM and its prospects for the future.

These are IBM's basic business beliefs under the Watsons:

Watson's IBM Basic Beliefs & Mgt Principles

As you all know, we [IBM] have long held to three basic beliefs in the conduct of this business: Respect for the individual, the best customer service and superior accomplishment of all tasks.

These beliefs, combined with IBM management principles, express the goals we seek, the means we use to achieve them, and the obligations we accept along the way.

These ideas don't change. We mean to keep them and we mean to live by them. Because we have grown so fast in the past few years and because we have so many new managers I thought it would be well for us to reissue the statement of our beliefs and principles.

In reissuing this document, we have combined the basic beliefs and the management principles into one compact statement, but the three basic beliefs — in the individual, in service, and in excellence — retain a special place and a special significance. They are the ones that provide every IBMer, whatever his job, daily guidance in his work and in his relationships with other IBMers and customers.

I hope you will study these principles, know them well, and discuss them with the people you manage.

Basic Concepts—IBM Principles

An organization, like an individual, must build on a bedrock of sound beliefs if it is to survive and succeed. It must stand by these beliefs in conducting its business. Every manager must live by these beliefs in the actions he takes and in the decisions he makes. The beliefs that guide IBM activities are expressed as IBM Principles.

Respect for the Individual

Our basic belief is respect for the individual, for his rights and dignity. It follows from this principle that IBM should:

1. Help each employee to develop his potential and make the best use of his abilities.
2. Pay and promote on merit.
3. Maintain two-way communications between manager and employee, with opportunity for a fair hearing and equitable settlement of disagreements.

Service to the Customer

We are dedicated to giving our customers the best possible service. Our products and services bring profits only to the degree that they serve the customer and satisfy his needs. This demands that we:

1. Know our customers' needs, and help them anticipate future needs.
2. Help customers use our products and services in the best possible way.
3. Provide superior equipment maintenance and supporting services.

Excellence Must Be a Way of Life

We want IBM to be known for its excellence. Therefore, we believe that every task, in every part of the business, should be performed in a superior manner and to the best of our ability. Nothing should be left to chance in our pursuit of excellence. For example, we must:

1. Lead in new developments.
2. Be aware of advances made by others, better them where we can, or be willing to adopt them whenever they fit our needs.
3. Produce quality products of the most advanced design and at the lowest possible cost.

IBM was successful because people – IBMers and IBM customers felt good about IBM and the people, even IBM customers worked hard to assure a two-way relationship. The Watsons believed in both *please and thank you;* and they loved to say: "nice job." That was my IBM. I always wanted to do my best.

Think of a company force of 400,000 employees feeling the way I did about Watson's IBM. Most employees were just like me because IBM treated us specially. As part of the new IBM a look at the Watson philosophy is a must.

Check out this letter from Tom Watson Jr. just before he retired:

Recognition

> *IBMers have always thrived on solving problems. Whether working in the customer's office, on the production line or in the laboratory, we have tried to look at problems as opportunities in disguise — opportunities to satisfy the customer, improve our skills and make the business grow.*

> *I hope IBM people never lose this characteristic.*

> *At the same time, we have always tried to remember that people provide the solutions. We should never become so preoccupied with solving problems that we forget the contributions of people.*

> *For the manager, this means putting the individual first. When your people do a good job, promptly tell them so. The phone call, the letter of appreciation, the personal "thank you" — these day-by-day relationships are the heart and soul of our business.*

> *Golden Circles, Hundred Percent Clubs, Outstanding Contribution Awards are important, but they are no substitute for telling someone, in your own personal terms, that he has done a first-rate job and you appreciate it.*

> *Money and title alone are not enough to satisfy the kinds of people that make IBM great. What counts most of all is*

the knowledge that individual contributions are recognized and valued. We all want to receive that sort of recognition, and we must all be quick to give it, too.

I believe you'll find, in most cases, that if you give thoughtful care to your people, they can take care of the problems.

Thomas J. Watson, Jr.
March 1970

Gerstner could have been born a Watson

Lou Gerstner came to IBM in 1993 just after I had left. I think it was fortuitous that Thomas Watson, Jr. picked Gerstner up at the airport on his first day of work on April 1, 1993, and the two enjoyed a nice chat before Gerstner went to work.

Gerstner had never gotten to enjoy the great IBM that many of us loved and he did not have an easy time as did the CEOs right after the Watsons. He did not have IBM's traditional cash hoard and in fact he inherited an IBM Company that was almost bankrupt. I suspect Watson and Gerstner discussed that among many things during the drive.

Lou Gerstner had it tough but he had a lot of Watson in him and he was a very good manager in many ways like the Watsons. He had to fire a lot of IBM employees but he also saved IBM from itself. Here are some words from Gerstner that are similar to those of Watson. I think you will see the type of character that I think is needed at the top of IBM for big Blue to make its comeback to the top.

Win, Execute and Team

All successful companies have good strategies. They all have good processes. They reward people for the right things. For the companies that truly break through, it comes down to their people. For us, it's not a question of talent. We have the best people in the industry. I knew that before I came to IBM, and I know it today. But are our people going to stretch to their potential — step up and lead? That's the real issue for IBM. What's really important is the personal commitment that each of us makes about how we're going to behave, how much we care, how much we're willing to give, how much we're willing to learn and adapt, what we think about every day that drives what we do operationally.

It comes back to win, execute and team. Those are not slogans or even institutional values. They are personal commitments. They're not things of the head, they're things of the heart and the gut. They are behavioral, not intellectual. You do not get up every morning and salute them. You get up every morning and live them. We have completed, for the most part, the task of restructuring the institution. Our success now is going to be a function of personal behavior — the behavior of each and every one of us.

Louis V. Gerstner, Jr.
1998

Chapter 9   Preparing to Work for IBM

Being an IBMer was always a great thing

I think it is appropriate in a book about helping IBM back to #1 again to talk about my own experience as an IBMer, and why the IBM-way can make many people want to do their best for a company such as IBM.

I wrote my first program in the Fortran language in 1965. It was during the summer after I graduated from E. L. Meyers High School in Wilkes-Barre, PA. I had been honored with a King's College Scholarship of $500.00 for the year and a $400.00 National Defense Student Loan.

Tuition at King's at the time was $950 a year. To make up the other $50.00 in tuition and the cost of books, I was given a job on campus for 40 hrs / week for the entire summer. It was continued during the semesters when the hours were reduced to 15 per week. I made $1.25 per hour under this program known as the Work-Study Program.

I worked in the maintenance department and my primary job each day was to clean three sets of steps from the top of the building to the basement. In the afternoon, along with my cohorts, I was assigned to various and sundry menial tasks across the institution, including for example, scraping the gum off the bottom of the tables in the King's College Library. At the end of the day, just like the regular maintenance staff, I was glad to be on my way home. Nothing came easy!

During my time in maintenance, Barry Strittmatter had become the King's IT Director and I got to know Barry well from working on two sets of steps which were in proximity to the King's Computing Center. Barry liked me as a person and he found a book in the Computing Center about Fortran. Knowing I was to be a Data Processing Major, he gave it to me to study.

I read the book from cover to cover and wrote my first program during that summer. Barry showed me how to keypunch the program into 80-column cards and he permitted me to use the IBM 026 keypunch to prepare my four statement Fortran program. The program added two numbers and printed a result.

He ran the program for me on the King's computer which was rented from the IBM Corporation. The machine was a second generation IBM 1620 Scientific Computer System. It had an IBM 1622 Card Read Punch and two IBM 1311 Disk Drives that used removable Disk Packs. The program worked. I was thrilled. I could not wait for the semester to begin in September. Through hard work, I had an edge. I had no idea what to expect.

Over the years, I was in the second graduating class of Data Processing Majors. My friend Paul Shovlin, who later became a full-time faculty member at King's was the first student to graduate in the program. Paul was two years ahead of me. He was in the King's class of 1967. However, he opted to change his major and he stayed an extra semester to gain enough credits for a Data Processing Degree. He graduated in January 1968. The class of 1968 graduated in May, and then my class, the class of 1969 graduated in May 1969.

In my freshman year, I got to spend a lot of time in the Computing Center doing work for faculty members who served as consultants for local businesses. When I began my second year with the maintenance department at King's, on a given day, I was again in the library scraping gum. Out of nowhere, Barry Strittmatter called me from under the table and he asked me if I would like a job in the Computing Center. Of course I said yes. I could not ask for more.

My first job in the Computing center as I still recall was to rip out the wires from some control panels and arrange the wires by color, which also happened to be by length. After gum assignments and dirty steps for over a year, the wire sorting assignment was just fine by me. After a while, I gained familiarity with the IBM 085 Collator, 082 Sorter, and the 514 Reproducing Punch, as well as the 407 Accounting Machine. Soon I was wiring boards for all of these machines.

Working in the King's Computing Center was a special job. I was learning my future profession and I got to meet a lot of IBM guys. The first two guys from IBM that I first met were Tom Balon, and John Faggotti. They were crackerjack IBM Customer Engineers (CEs). They wore suits. They were repair guys and they wore regular business suits with white shirts and ties. I was amazed that a repair man would be wearing a business suit, tie, and white shirt. IBM had its ways.

They talked about IBM all the time and what a great job they had and I learned what a great company IBM was for which to work. They told me about the IBM golf course in Endicott, and the IBM family dinners and the idea of respect for the individual. I was impressed with them and with IBM. I was just seventeen years old when we met. Their enthusiasm for IBM rubbed off. Who would not like IBM?

There were a number of other IBMers that I got to meet. Pete Kozochoke was the IBM salesman for King's and Tony Opalski was the IBM Systems Engineer. They all worked out of the local Branch Office in Scranton but the CES had a sub-office in Wilkes-Barre where they hung around sometimes like Maytag Repairmen waiting for a call. IBM saved time and money by not sending these guys back to Scranton between calls.

I took tons of job interviews when I was a senior at King's. Many recruiters came to King's looking for computer specialists. I passed up jobs with Nestles, Bell Labs, Shell Oil, NCR and others after I had my interview with IBM.

It turns out that Tony Opalski was a member of my Church and he would talk to me after Mass on Sundays telling me more and more about IBM. I wanted to take as many job interviews with as many companies as I could. When the college baseball season began, I slowed down the away job interviews. Tony kept telling me to not bother, I was going to work for IBM. He really helped me.

George Mohanco, a fellow senior DP Major at King's and I went to IBM in Utica, NY for an overnight trip right before baseball season. We met SE Manager Jim Harper, top salesman Dick "Bucky" Flint, and Systems Engineers Ken Cloud and Ken Sayers.

We made customer calls all day to various IBM systems accounts in Utica. Again, I was very impressed and so was George. We both got job offers to start as Systems Engineers on June 23, 1969. Neither George nor I were sure about accepting jobs yet as we had a few interviews left. Tony Opalski kept encouraging me.

Two other King's seniors took jobs with IBM and we discussed their reasons. Joe Grant had taken a job with Kodak but got sick and they withdrew the job offer so Joe interviewed with IBM and they offered him a nice job in Rochester, NY in their computer laboratory.

Dennis Grimes also went to Rochester, NY as a large systems—Assistant Systems Engineer. It was not long after our interviews that George and I accepted our small-systems—Assistant Systems Engineer positions with IBM in Utica. George and I got our training in the same IBM schools whereas Joe and Dennis went to large IBM systems schools.

One of the arguments that Tony Opalski used on me when I was indifferent about IBM came after he had asked me if I really felt I knew a lot about computers. I admitted that I did not think I knew an awful lot and that I knew little about current line technology such as the IBM System/360, which had recently become available.

Tony smiled and he said that in the first eighteen months with IBM in order to become a Systems Engineer, the company would spend tons of money on my education. He said that I would be in formal IBM education classes and on the job training working with experienced Systems Engineers (SEs) at IBM client DP shops.

He estimated the value of the education at well over $100,000. I was already thinking IBM would be the place to get a job for me and the value of the education sure made it even that more appealing. Mohanco was ready to go and we were talking.

As and aside, when Dennis Grimes graduated from his first ten week CST (large systems training) in Washington, DC, a head hunter approached him while the two were enjoying a libation. The head hunter offered Dennis a job on the spot without even asking his college grades. That was the perceived value of the training delivered by IBM.

For George M. and me, our training began right after a two-week branch office orientation in Utica. We had a number of self-studies to work through before we could go to class. Nobody wanted to be sent home for not passing the class entry exam. Our first day in the branch office was very historic. IBM announced unbundling. This affected George and I and Dennis big time. We were too fresh to understand exactly what had happened.

Unbundling # 1 -- 1969

Unbundling historically is noted as one of IBM's most important and most controversial decisions. We discussed other aspects of unbundling in Chapter 1. IBM rental customers received a "whopping" three percent discount and were notified that other than mutually planned support—planned prior to June 23, 1969—Systems Engineers were no longer free. My first day of work was June 23, 1969, and at the big meeting, I learned how much my job and everybody else's had changed.

Customers also learned at the formal IBM announcement on June 23, 1969 that they would no longer see their friendly Systems Engineers on a regular bass unless they paid a fee. In other words, system support from IBM was no longer free. This did not go over well with IBM customers. The surprise factor made it even worse. IBM hoped customers did not notice but they did!

To enforce this new rule internally, IBM local managers did not permit Systems Engineers to leave the office during the business day unless they had a paying services customer and they were working on the contract. This did not work out too well and eventually as customers balked. SEs were subtly permitted back into accounts by IBM on the QT, and there was little talk about billing the customer.   IBM could not live with the rigors of the decision.

IBM education / training for IBMers and for customers was second to none #1

Besides a number of one and two-week classes, IBM sent me to two big classes in New York City called Basic Data Processing I, and Basic Data Processing II. They were five weeks and seven weeks respectively, separated by three months of field OJT.

The first class focused on board wiring and computer / TAB equipment applications. The second class was about computer hardware and how to program in Report Program Generator I and II, FORTRAN, and COBOL. We learned about the System/360 Model 20 (RPG I) and the IBM 1130 (RPG II & Fortran) Scientific System. RPG was a new language at the time.

During our second class, IBM announced the System/3 model 10 which used a 96-column card that was 1/3 the size of the standard 80-column card. It was so new that IBM training modules did not include it.

Before I went to Army Basic training, I got to wire an Aged Trial Balance 402 board at a CPA account in Rome, NY, and I wrote a number of RPG programs for Carl's Drugs, a new account in Utica at the time.

In December, I went to Army Basic Training and resumed my IBM career again in May 1970 in Utica after having become a Private First Class (E3) in the Utica National Guard. That meant I had one top stripe and one rounded bar to show my rank. When I met George at the reception center, I was a Private (E2) with one chevron.

Ironically, when George got out of his Army training six weeks after me, IBM in Scranton, our home town office, offered him a transfer from Utica, which he accepted. That summer he and I met up again in Washington for a seven week intensive computer training course. We learned about operating systems – IBM System/360 DOS and small mainframes.

Almost immediately upon my return, I was assigned to a new System/3 installation at the A. Barton. Hepburn Hospital in Ogdensburg, New York. My job was to implement a brand new IBM System 3 card-only system for Patient Billing, Revenue Accounting, and Accounts Receivable. By the time

I finished my work at the hospital, I was transferred to the Scranton IBM Office—my home town.

George and I met up again in Scranton. The rest of my twenty-three years with IBM were with IBM in Scranton, PA, though I was offered a number of promotions over the years. I chose to stay in Scranton close by my family. Eventually after he got married in 1976, George Mohanco transferred to Atlanta and Dennis Grimes transferred from NY into Scranton as a Data Base / Data Communications expert.

Having been trained in IBM's smaller system – S/360 Model 20 and the 1130, and then System/3, when IBM decided to create a new small computer division that included manufacturing, services, systems, and marketing, I was a natural for inclusion in the IBM General Systems Division. It is documented that IBM Chairman Thomas Watson Jr. created this division in many ways because the government was threatening to break up IBM. Watson, Learson and Chairman Frank Cary were hoping to create a natural way of splitting the company if the government's axe fell. If IBM were to be split, there would be IBM and GSD. I was destined for GSD.

The IBM Company established the IBM General Systems Division (GSD), headquartered in Atlanta in 1969. Rochester, Minnesota became one of its two principal manufacturing and development sites. At the time, Don Stephenson was named general manager of Rochester. Art Becker, my friend Bonnie Becker's father started the Rochester plant for IBM's T.J. Watson Jr. Watson was a frequent dinner guest at the Becker home so Bonnie and her brother Art Jr. surely had a privileged childhood. Art Becker was one of Watson's key personnel and personal friends, who had the wherewithal and the smarts to create an IBM plant from scratch.

Chapter 10 The IBM Company Was Haunted by an Anti-Trust Law Suit.

GSD would have been the "other IBM"

If there is one thing that I liked more than IBM itself was the General Systems Division (GSD) of IBM. Formed originally as a manufacturing and development arm for smaller system, the role of GSD was expanded and it entered the IBM Sales Branch Offices. I originally worked for the Data Processing Division of IBM. DPD sold all IBM equipment to all IBM customers. With GSD being a company within a company, the sales personnel who were responsible for selling and installing new accounts with IBM's small business systems were moved from DPD to GSD.

GSD was initially formed in 1969. At that time, as noted all IBM marketing was done by DPD. Then in 1972, IBM began to change marketing. It split the Data Processing Division into two divisions, GSD and DPD. By 1974, GSD was given its own marketing arm. It took some time but in 1975, GSD was not such a small little company.

In 1975, IBM had 4500 Sales Representatives were working out of 67 local branch offices plus another 3000 field service representatives, a group which IBM called Customer Engineers, were split out from the Field Service Division and they became the service arm of GSD. This was no small business enterprise.

It helps to recall that IBM had become a giant in the electronic data processing field as it was called then by the mid-1950s. IBM computers were introduced and the

company was preparing to transition its product line to
computers. But, all of IBM's success to the mid-1950 had
come in the punch-card tabulating machine rental business
that Watson Sr. had built in the 1930s.

IBM always projected an image as offering superior products
at a lower price than its competitors. IBM customers were
portrayed as loyal and satisfied with the service provided by
"Big Blue." My own observations suggest that this was not
just a portrayal, it was a reality.

IBM's success, particularly with the market dominance
brought about by the introduction of the Company's
System/360, was a cause for distrust and suspicion by both
its competitors and the federal government. IBM was starting
to look like a monopoly in the computer business which
ironically did not exist until the 1950's.

A preliminary inquiry was made in the mid-1960s by the U.S.
Department of Justice as to what it believed might be
antitrust violations by IBM. The complaint for the case U.S.
v. IBM was filed in U.S. District Court, Southern District of
New York on January 17, 1969 by the Justice Department.
Coincidentally, IBM formed its General Systems Division in
1969.

The anti-trust suit alleged that IBM violated the Section 2 of
the Sherman Act by monopolizing or attempting to
monopolize the general purpose electronic digital computer
system market, specifically computers designed primarily for
business. Unlike the Microsoft suit in recent years, IBM took
this very seriously and dedicated substantial resources to fight
these allegations. Thousands of IBMers worked on this
lawsuit.

There were several charges against IBM. The government
contended that IBM planned to and did eliminate emerging
competition that threatened the erosion of IBM's monopoly
power by devising and executing business strategies which
were not illegal, but which did not provide users with a better

price, a better product or better service. Specifically, it was alleged that IBM had hindered the development of service and peripherals competitors by maintaining a single price policy for its machines, software and support services.

In other words when you rented from IBM you received the ability to go to IBM schools, free manuals, free Systems Engineering Support, Free parts, Free Customer Engineers to fix the system, and free software from a library which IBM kept for its customers. This idea was called bundling and the more bundling was heard in IBM circles the more concerned the company as that it might have to address that aspect of the lawsuit before others.

Besides bundling, to assure a fresh crop of college graduates that were familiar with how to work with IBM equipment, the Company had granted discounts for universities and other educational institutions. By so doing, it was alleged that IBM influenced those institutions to select IBM computers.

Moreover, it was charged that IBM had introduced underpriced models knowing that they could not be produced on time and did this to prevent the placement of competitors' machines. For example, IBM had prematurely announced new systems such as various models of System/360 claiming that they were superior products, noting their availability was imminent when in fact, it took several years for completion and certain models were canceled. IBM had great concern as the penalty which was discussed besides fines was the demand that the company be broken into smaller pieces.

The trial began May 19, 1975 and spanned a period of over six years. Incidentally, within calendar year 1995, GSD had completed its sales division transition and became a fully operational business within the IBM Corporation. Coincidence?

After thousands of hours of testimony (testimony of over 950 witnesses, 87 in court, the remainder by deposition) and the submission of tens of thousands of exhibits, the case was withdrawn by William F. Baxter, assistant attorney general in charge of the Antitrust Division, Department of Justice, on January 8, 1982. Baxter signed a Stipulation of Dismissal that stated the government's charges were "without merit" It was later discovered that Baxter had failed to disclose that he had been retained as a consultant to a West Coast law firm defending IBM in private antitrust cases.

Baxter had reviewed the case and met with both sides in 1981. His reasoning for dismissing the case was that the Antitrust Division's view regarding Section 2 violations had evolved since the commencement of the suit; the government was backing off antitrust actions. Baxter believed that the cost of continuation would be too high and that the government was unlikely to win the case. Baxter maintained that IBM had achieved its large market share legally without resorting to predatory practices, and that Section 2 could not filed against a company because of its success.

For those interested in reading more about the anti-trust lawsuit, there is a great reference piece available: http://findingaids.hagley.org/xtf/view?docId=ead/1980.xml

IBM GSD had become a very successful company within IBM. Its major product was the System/38 and the AS/400 was in the long-term planning stages. Mainframe IBM still dominated the company and this little lab in Rochester was looked upon with enmity by those in the DPD marketing division as well as the divisions that controlled IBM's huge water cooled and air-cooled mainframe computer systems. As successful as GSD and its products were, they were viewed as rogue by establishment IBM and it was feared that without the antitrust suit, GSD's wares would somehow disappear and the mainframe decisions would fill the bill.

From my vantage point, from what I saw myself and from opinions of other marketing representatives and systems engineers who at various times employed by both divisions and sold both sets of products over time, GSD was a better run company than IBM. It had to be to survive against all of the constraints placed upon it by Mother IBM, which had a definite mainframe bias.

It is tough to imagine that the little division had the best management and the most advanced computer system in the universe (System/38 – FS). More difficult to image I regret to say is that those responsible for profit in the IBM Corporation did not use those two facts to the company's advantage. Instead, they played their bench-level managers and their second best system line as if it were their best.

Without getting into any of the specifics of the IBM PC, IBM had similar disdain for this innovation and success from non-mainframe division products. As we all have seen, after creating a PC monopoly, IBM lost almost all of its PC market share within the first five years. When big Blue decided to take the PC back with the introduction of the PS/2, it was already too far gone.

IBM had left the barn door open and the Clones plus Microsoft and Intel walked right in. I like to call it mainframe myopia. Such myopia and elite stodginess still exists to an extent in Big Blue. For IBM to succeed and be #1 in the future, to make my dream come true, IBM needs to overcome its penchant for destroying great ideas.

It took just a short while for IBM to completely dismantle the General Systems Division as a threat to mainframe IBM. The company created two marketing organizations to make its sales force more efficient. I was with IBM at the time in 1982 - 1983, and was asked to join the National Marketing Division which was designated to sell smaller hardware. In 1985, with IBM was supposedly worried about a proliferation of small computer systems which were seen as threatening to squeeze profits, IBM got rid of the two divisions and merged them into the National Accounts Division.

IBM took some bows to the press when they noted that management expected that this particular elimination of GSD residue would significantly trim I.B.M.'s overhead. GSD was a focused division, especially in marketing and leaving everything to the big guys in the National Accounts Division marked the end of IBM's being able to sell new accounts.

Under the reorganization, each field office was empowered to sell every I.B.M. product - from typewriters to mainframe computers - to all of the companies within its territory. Previously, from a prior reorganization which began the GSD demise, the National Accounts division, dealt with I.B.M.'s biggest customers, and another, the National Marketing division, dealt with smaller businesses. Under the plan that took at the beginning of that year, the divisions were merged and then split geographically: one took care of customers in the Northeast and Middle West; another will handle those in the South and West.

The New York Times summed it up:

"Before 1981, its sales force specialized in specific products, some selling mainframes and others concentrating on smaller systems. As minicomputers and personal computers proliferated, however, the system confused customers, who often had to deal with a host of I.B.M. sales representatives. More importantly, it left no one I.B.M. sales representative responsible for integrating disparate systems, a growing problem as corporations move to tie all their computers into seamless networks.

Since that initial reorganization, which led to major relocations and new training programs, I.B.M.'s sales force has been free to sell the company's entire line to customers. But old habits continued, and some I.B.M. officials have privately acknowledged the company should be doing far better in installing small equipment at the nation's largest companies."

I know that the Gray Lady thinks what they printed was true but it is a biased view from the managers that made the decision. In essence, once everybody could sell everything, nobody wanted to sell the small stuff. Moreover, IBM began to use distributors. IBM would sell a system and local management would not accept the order unless the Salesman who owned the territory would swear the system was sold by a distributor.

Then, the distributor got a bigger commission than the IBM person who sold it. IBM rigged the numbers so it could eliminate its national sales force. Now, as previously noted, few distributors even attempt to sell IBM to new accounts. It was just another way for IBM to minimize the smaller systems that had become so successful while GSD was in operation.

The Times interview said what I just said with some IBM spin. It was intended not to work and it did not work. I was there. IBM is still in the toilet for decisions such as this made in the John Opel / John Akers time frame.

"Mr. Rogers [Once GSD President] contended yesterday that those economic changes had little to do with the reorganization. But analysts said the new structure paved the way for the company to concentrate its own sales force on the most profitable business, and to spin off smaller sales to third parties [aka distributors].

"I.B.M.'s sales force itself can no longer afford to make one-on-one calls to sell typewriters, personal computers and copiers," said Thomas J. Crotty, an analyst for the Gartner Group. "The margins are just not there."

Actually, IBM could not afford to give its business to distributors. That other people than IBMers would hold customer loyalty was a false premise. Only IBM employees were loyal to IBM. I saw it firsthand.

Before it was all over for IBM in new accounts, the distributors were selling Dell, HP, Gateway, and just about every Wintel product made to the exclusion of IBM's products. The Brainiacs at IBM that decided that third parties would save money obviously did not have mandatory loyalty training for its distributors.

IBMers worked hard for IBM because we loved working for the company and we loved helping make the company successful. And, yes, we loved the recognition also. For our hard work, many were fired and others were forced to leave through other means.

Chapter 11 Dear IBM Make My Dream Happen!

For IBM to be #1, the dream must come true

It is nice to dream. When you look at what I have been saying about the old IBM being part of a new IBM is just good business. IBM needs to treat its people better and promise to be a better company. Then, employees will voluntarily give 200% even if it means sometimes missing a picnic on the Fourth of July.

Another was IBM can begin the transition to a better people company is to bring some development back from overseas. Many people think IBM is an All-American Company because Big Blue has controlled the press on what it has been doing with its work force. Bring people back. Pay a fair wage, and give Americans jobs. After employees begin to trust the company again, IBM must make sure that it adopts the Watsonian Beliefs. They are not hard to come by. They are a model for great companies all over the world and they are on the Internet and many are in this book.

The Board of Directors needs to watch its top managers better and needs to take its job more seriously. I have seen reasonably high managers in IBM making decisions which help them personally rather than the company. The Board has to ask itself how IBM today is not be of the trillion dollar PC industry that it created and only one CEO ever got fired. How many Board members were fired over this manor stockholder loss?

The Board of IBM needs to be educated on technology at a human level. If the Board does not come to the classes, the Board needs to get fired. IBM management should never have had the opportunity to mess up IBM as much as the post Watson group, especially John Opel but surely we must include John Akers. Akers got fired but IBM is still losing money today.

IBM can stop losing money if it chooses to highlight its silent weapon, the Future System as available today, thirty-eight years after the System/38 in the embodiment of an IBM Power System with the IBM I Operating system. This is the 2020 AS/400.

When you answer the question about who else could have invested seven years effort plus the FS Design before it and then bring in the finest IBM experts to finish the system, you will know the answer to why it has not been duplicated. Nobody even Microsoft could afford to build such an elegant operating system?

Some say that only IBM could have created the FS (System/38, AS/400, and Power i) and only IBM could destroy the system by ignoring it. No company besides IBM could have invested as much capital on the technology that was necessary to create the AS/400, and no other company could intentionally destroy the product of IBM's efforts—the finest computer system ever built.

After many years spent telling customers that the company really was planning to promote the AS/400, the plan never came. IBM's AS/400 customers are now in a quiet revolt against the company. IBM could have done a great job in its vital roles as caretaker and life-sustainer of this system, upon which many customers run their businesses. Instead IBM was pleased with its existing customers and not moving the machine to new accounts and mainframe shops preserved IBM's mainframe business If IBM had doing a good job in promoting the best system in its arsenal, one of the most asked questions in the industry would not be the following:

"Is the AS/400 Dead?"

Most people see IBM as a very successful company that is really great at making big computers. That is IBM's legacy for those who drink from the fountain of public knowledge. Unless you work in the computer industry, you would naturally be unaware of all the ventures over the years in which IBM was less than successful.

IBM is asked the question quite often. I have summarized below IBM's last documented response to the question given at the AS/400's 25th birthday party in 2013. Technically, this piece below which again is a summary, might be called a rebuttal to my contention that IBM does not do enough for its AS/400 line. Here we go:

> Some server operating systems were built to last the test of time. The System/38 which became the IBM AS/400 which became the Power I is one such system.
>
> The AS/400 (Application System/400) was first introduced by IBM going on 30 years ago in June of 1988. Though its epitaph has been written many times, it is a system that is still alive and well today. The core server operating system that delivered the smarts to the AS/400 is still alive under the name IBM i, IBM now calls the AS/400 its Power System with IBM i. I call it Power i or AS/400.
>
> Though the Power System hardware and the Power chip are now built separately from the operating system, the "I" in IBM i still stands for integration. The AS/400 is by far the easiest system to use and program in the galaxy. The AS/400 OS from its birth almost 30 years ago has always been an integrated operating system that includes an integrated data base with a name—DB2.

IBM believes that the biggest change to the platform occurred in 2008, when the IBM i operating system was brought together with IBM's AIX Unix operating system and Linux onto the same Power server systems. The same IBM Power chip now drives AIX, Linux, and IBM I (AS/400).

IBM celebrated the 25th birthday of the AS/400 just a few years ago at which time IBM noted that it does recognize some of the special ingredients in the AS/400—namely the technology-independent machine interface. This is an FS concept which has enabled the system to continue to grow without rewriting the operating system or application programs. Think about Windows to get a feel for how substantial an advantage that is.

The continuing promise of the IBM i is that it is able to change as underlying hardware changes without disruption. It's a promise that could see the platform survive for the next 25 years. IBM can add one more ingredient if it chooses to be # 1. It can make the machine pervasive. Wherever you go there can be an AS/400 and that would make computing all across the spectrum much easier than it is today. IBM's Ian Jarman sums it up with:

"I'm very confident given that we made a big promise of technology independence 25 years ago with the AS/400 and we delivered on that promise, I'm very confident that people will be running IBM i applications 25 years from now." Now, if we can get IBM to do some advertising about what this is, that would be very nice.

As nice as IBM spokesman can be regarding IBM's great plans, Big Blue has had a tough time delivering on promises, both made and implied.

For the record, today's IBM is the same IBM that lost the entire PC business, the relational database business, the telecommunications business, the application software business, the satellite communications business, the Unix business, the word processing business, the video disk business, the computerized branch exchange business, the disk drive business, as well a number of other businesses in which you and I would have made millions.

Yet, without learning a lesson, the current IBM is behaving similarly to its checkered past with its AS/400 customers as it did during these other great losses. What are we to expect? IBM can be #1 again but it needs a strong weapon. The Future System (FS), originally built as the System/38 plus some good management is the IBM ticket back to #1.

Rather than waiting until it is too late, IBM's AS/400 customers have been quite outspoken to IBM and to the industry. These customers are adamant that the company must do something to promote the machine. Make it pervasive. However, until the current earnings slide, "IBM knows best" has been the company's mantra as it continues a forced march against an undisclosed plan that seems to include minimizing the positive impact of the Future System (FS) on its bottom line. IBM can do lots better if it tries. .

In order to make my points about the AS/400 / FS story in many of the books I have written about IBM, I have reached back through a lot of IBM history. Some of the history I lived through as an IBM branch office systems engineer. Some I lived through as an IBM customer, and some as an industry consultant. Though I have not seen it all yet, I've seen enough to know that sound marketing logic is not the prevailing thought in the current IBM. Think Signs and Think Pads are not seen very often today in IBM, and there is good reason. I want the new IBM to be a thinking IBM.

Besides the books I have written asking IBM to make better decisions, I have written many how-to books about the AS/400 from WebSphere to application development to DB2 database on to RPG programming. Here is a sampling of the

books that I have written about IBM, hoping to get the
company to make the right marketing decisions:

- **Chip Wars**
- **Can the AS/400 Survive IBM?**
- **Thanks You IBM**: *The story of how IBM helped today's
  technology billionaires and millionaires gain their vast
  fortunes*
- **The All-Everything Machine**
- **The All-Everything Operating System**
- **Whatever happened to the IBM AS/400?**
- **I Had a Dream that IBM Could Be # 1 Again**

This is not a technical book. However, there are a few areas
in which I do get just a little bit technical, hoping that I can
show the reader in reasonably simple terms how the AS/400
is a special machine with a long and successful tradition.
Though this book is nonfiction, there may be some areas in
which my analysis of a situation differs from IBM's.

Moreover, there are surely areas in which my recollection of
facts and actual events may be different from IBM's. Of
course, I believe that my analysis and my recollections are
accurate, and that's why I wrote the book from my
perspective, not from IBM's. My AS/400 customers and I
believe that we have already had enough of IBM's
perspective. It has not worked.

When you finish reading this book, you may think that I have
treated IBM and its management team somewhat harshly. I
ask for your indulgence. That I was motivated after a real
dream to write a book of on how IBM can be # 1 again gives
you an idea of how harshly I believe IBM has treated its FS
customers and consultants, and how much I want IBM to
succeed and hit the top again using the results of FS as its
major tool.

If you have a chance, please attend a stockholder meeting some time and speak up about how you think IBM can be # 1 again and how you think it can get there.

At any rate, I hope that at the very least, along with learning a number of things, you enjoy reading this book. I sure have enjoyed writing it.

I think I made my case. IBM needs good management and an ample injection of Watson's basic beliefs. It also needs a secret weapon to wipe out the competition. That weapon is the Future System designed almost fifty years ago and still weaponized to blow all other systems out of the universe. So, IBM needs to look for the best architecture on the planet and it will be found in the IBM storehouse. The Power i System of today is that FS brought forward to today. IBM must use it to become # 1 in technology again.

Rather than repeat myself about topical areas that I have covered in other books, I have included a number of chapters with the particular book references. Here they come in normal chapter numbering sequence:

Chapter 12   IBM and the Power i

From the Book: *What Happened to the IBM AS/400?*
Chapter 3   Who's on First?

The Best Computer Ever

The AS/400 is the best and the most special computer ever
built. That is why it is inconceivable that the company that
owns the rights to the machine does not seem to try to earn a
huge profit from it. For you music lovers out there, it may
help to know that the AS/400 is to computers what Bose is to
great sound. Bring on the music.

As the direct descendent of the System/38, the AS/400 is
even more wonderful. The older System/38 line was not as
well-endowed performance-wise. In fact, it suffered from
capacity constraints imposed by IBM's own mainframe
division. However, it was built with the same advanced
architecture, and thus, by design, is the same high tech
machine as the AS/400. Therefore, I would argue that the
AS/400 and the System/38 are singularly the finest
computers that any company has ever made.

AS/400 Becomes eServer Power i

In the fall of 2000, as noted in Chapter 2, IBM changed the
name of the AS/400 to the eServer Power i 400. Many who
earn their livelihoods from AS/400-related work have chosen
to recognize the Power i not as a different computer but a
branding change. That change, unfortunately, has done more
to hurt the prospects of attracting more computer users to the
AS/400 platform than to help it. The corporate rumor mill

suggests that a new name may be in order for the platform in the near future. That would be a good idea. Hopefully, the corporate "namers" will buy a few thinking caps before they try again.

Tell Somebody!

IBM's legions of AS/400 customers have been crying out to the company for some help in giving the AS/400 product line some name recognition among regular people. They are not happy having to do IBM's marketing job in their own IT shops. Having to continually justify the AS/400 as being more capable than Windows and UNIX is a tiring chore.

IBM has reacted indifferently to its customers' plea for help, and the rebranding is a major manifestation of that lack of concern. When IBM placed the eServer brand on each of its four server lines, it made the AS/400 appear as merely another horse in IBM's eServer stable. The new branding message is that the AS/400 (Power i) is no better and no worse than any of IBM's other horses. But that is not true! Nothing in the branding or the message gives a prospective new computer an idea about whether the box is a packhorse, a thoroughbred, a workhorse, a show horse, a mule, or a plain old jackass.

Anyone who takes the time to look would see a machine that is the embodiment of all that IBM knows about computers, implemented with an elegance unparalleled in the computing era. The reason why IBM chooses to downplay its finest system is an enigma. The fact that IBM minimizes the system, however, is indisputable.

Only IBM Could Create an AS/400

Only a big company with such huge resources as IBM could have conceived, designed, and built such an elegant machine. For this, I must thank the IBM Corporation. But the thanking ends at the moment of its birth. The record shows that the AS/400 has narrowly escaped death a number of times from the hand of its very creator, IBM.

> "....the only thing I can say about IBM and the AS/400 is that it never would have been built without IBM ...no one could have afforded to build the S/38 and subsequently the 400. Granted it will never get its due from IBM because of the "eating your children" scenario...even now it would not survive without IBM technology behind it. It is stuck in a "hardware neutral world" with ever increasing "software neutral" components... ...UDB, SQL, TCP, Unix, SAP, Lotus etc...it will lose its uniqueness...It already has in hardware ... fortunately, I have my retirement and all I need is for the AS/400 to remain viable for the next 2 years and then for all I care it can disappear...."

That says something, doesn't it?

Credit for each word above is given to George Mohanco, who, like myself, began his IBM career on June 23, 1969, the day IBM announced "unbundling." And, like myself, when given the opportunity to leave IBM, protect his pension, get a nice financial send-off, and pursue another career, he took the first train out, in 1992.

George retired from the Pensacola, Florida, branch office when it existed in the early 1990s. And, like myself, on July 1, 1999, George finally began to collect from the IBM "eagle" each month, and we both expect this to last for quite a while, until we reach that place above, where we expect to find the AS/400 in charge of all operations, and to see some confused former IBM executive wondering why he hadn't thought of that while he was still on earth.

-- End of Chapter 3 Excerpt from Whatever Happened to the IBM AS/400--

Chapter 13   Computing--Easy with FS

From the Book: *What Happened to the IBM AS/400*
Chapter 5   It's a Beautiful Day in the Neighborhood?

Automatic Transmissions 'R' Us

From the very beginning, the AS/400 was designed to be simpler than all other systems. To this day, no other platform has such a good a balance between "easy-to-use" and "powerful." Unlike Mainframes, Windows, and Unix, the AS/400 comes without a clutch. It's got a fully functional automatic transmission. In fact, when you drive an AS/400, you would find that for the most part, you are not needed; the system drives itself.

You can know enough to run an IBM Power i or an AS/400 when you know less than a few percentages of what there is to know. Max Miller found that out quickly. With the AS/400, for example, much of what you want to do is already set up with default values, and thus, you do not have to think out each piece of a command. You just run it. With a minimal amount of training, one person can in fact know enough to run an entire company using an AS/400. It's done all the time. That's why once people have worked with an AS/400, with OS/400, they are spoiled and resent working again with other machines.

In basic no-frills form, the AS/400 is hard to beat for a new install of a reliable system at any new customer location. PCs are still for fluff things such as e-mail clients, drawings, and things requiring really cheap connectivity. You may not yet want to surf the Net on an AS/400, but you surely would not want to trust a fully audited, transaction-controlled, mission-critical invoicing application running on behalf of 100 users if it were written in a PC-oriented kids language, and if it were running on a farm of Windows PC servers with 20 label printers in multiple plants. For this, you need a nice sized professional staff if the application is for a PC-based system. Why would anybody do this with a PC-based system? If the system were an AS/400, just one person would be able to handle the mission, and the person would also be able to take lunch.

Part of how the AS/400 is able to get lots done in a reliable fashion is that it is much easier to use, and its rules are stricter than any other environment. Hackers don't like rules, so for the most part, they stay clear of the AS/400. On other platforms, for example, you can write a program that destroys the system itself. You can do it intentionally as a hacker, or you can do it by error, unintentionally, because you did something wrong.

Most of us have seen the ease with which viruses can be created on Windows systems and how hackers break into Windows and Unix boxes all the time. AS/400 prevents this within its architecture. It prevents users from killing themselves. It is not unimportant that the techno-geeks don't like it as much as they like Unix or Windows. They get stopped at the door. They can't hack the AS/400 and bring it down successfully--and they don't like that one bit!

Ease of Use for Technical Staff

AS/400 professionals love the ease with which they can manage the AS/400 system and its relational database facility. On mainframe computers and Unix boxes, and even Windows boxes, it is not quite so simple. For example, on all three of the non-AS/400 flavors, the database is not integrated. That means that you get to install it, apply the patches, and ensure that it is fully functional. You get to make sure that it works, and get to integrate it with everything else on your machine. Moreover, with mainframes, in order to have a database, you have to hire an expensive extra person to your staff. This new person is called a database administrator (DBA) and he comes with a price tag of about $80,000 or more per year.

A DBA is not just needed on a mainframe. When A PC server is used for real business applications, a DBA is required on this inexpensive platform as well. Moreover, on the PC platform, you always install in pairs, in case one goes down.

So you get to do the installation work twice. If you know of any advanced PC shops with databases that do not have a DBA, you know they're not doing too well. Though the AS/400 is a database machine, you need no DBA, because the database is built into the machine. Most programmers discover that they have been using a database long after their applications have been using it successfully with the AS/400 for years.

The AS/400 Keeps on Ticking

Internet and AS/400 oriented magazines have many wonderful stories about how AS/400s just go ahead and get their work done, regardless of the level of feeding and caring the systems get. The AS/400 is very much like a good old Timex watch. Sometimes, however, AS/400s keep on ticking long after they are forgotten. For example, this story relayed by Mark Villa of Charleston, South Carolina, is one that brings the ease of AS/400 operations picture well into focus.

"There was an AS/400 in a plant that was doing its thing on a regular basis, and it was basically unnoticed out in the plant. Unknowingly, the company built a wall in the area during some construction, and someone went hunting for the AS/400 months later, and found it was enclosed."

Runs Many Applications At Once

Unlike Windows Servers, AS/400s run many applications at the same time. Windows servers do not do well when used for more than one function. That's why a single-server PC grows into a small farm of PC servers almost overnight. An AS/400 can be a Web server, a Domino Notes server, a Java Virtual Machine, a Windows NT server, an OS/2 server, a firewall, an invoice machine, an accounts receivable machine, and so on--all on the same single-processor box, without even having to partition the unit. More industry analysts are noticing this facility and giving the AS/400 very high marks in their total-cost-of-computing analyses.

The AS/400 can actually be a server farm under its one set of covers with just one server box. It can also provide the same facility for Windows servers as a storage area network (SAN). Because the AS/400 is so many machines in one, sometimes it gets no credit for being any, when it is actually all. Today, IBM seems to have a problem with the identity of the AS/400. Back in 1988, the company had no problem spelling out exactly what an AS/400 was all about. The company highlighted the AS/400 as its workhorse of midrange servers. IBM called the AS/400 its midrange business system. It still is, but since the name change, IBM has forgotten.

Technical Note: A SAN is short for Storage Area Network. This is a modern notion involving the separation of the data storage elements from single computers and the centralization of that data on a central server, the role of which is storage management. A topology would show many servers all accessing data from the same set of disk drives managed by the Storage Server in the Storage Area Network. Because many Intel servers can be installed as blades in an AS/400, the AS/400 box itself serves as a SAN for Windows Servers at 10 to 15% of the cost of a typical SAN approach.

Today the AS/400, or Power i, or Power System with IBM I
is still alive and kicking, with an installed base of more than
400,000 and perhaps as many as 750,000 systems in about
250,000 businesses around the world. Between 30,000 and
90,000 new systems are sold each year, according to some
published statistics. The AS/400 survives because many of
its customers buy a new one every four or five years, and
because IBM has chosen not to eliminate the box--yet!

AS/400 Staying Power: Bring on the Clones!

There are serious concerns by some industry analysts about
the AS/400 platform's proprietary image and what is
perceived by most AS/400 customers as IBM's failure to
aggressively promote the platform. AS/400 customers want
the box to be successful, and they don't want to have to
explain to their management why they have an AS/400 each
time the lease is up. The fact that the AS/400 is still selling
to its existing customers flies in the face of long-standing
predictions about the demise of the platform. IBM's biggest
AS/400 problem today is that its customers are upset by the
way the company markets the box.

Today, no other company makes AS/400s. More than being
worried about AS/400 clones coming into being, IBM's
AS/400 faithful are concerned about IBM trying to abandon
support of AS/400's operating system, OS/400. Just as
Windows brings life to hundreds of millions of PCs, OS/400
is the lifeblood of the AS/400's midrange technical
capabilities.

IBM does not seem to like OS/400 (now IBM i), and in old
boxing terms, the company seems to have a favorite "bum of
the month" for the AS/400 to run against. At times IBM
favors Unix, and at other times it looks like Linux or
Windows. Rather than any of these has-beens, AS/400
shops would welcome some smart and savvy competitor

coming along with an AS/400 clone. If OS/400 is worth cloning, this would be viewed as a long-term positive prognosis for the platform.

The AS/400 constituency is not happy with IBM and its homogenization tactics and the "bum of the month" club. If a company, such as HP or Sun, appeared on the scene with a reasonably reliable copy of any hardware box running OS/400--a clone, if you will--you'd need to bring in MPs to direct traffic during the migration flow.

Old Reliable

The most cited reason behind the continuing popularity of the AS/400 is its reliability. The unprecedented ease of use and the low cost of management follow right behind. The AS/400 continues to be an out-of-the-box product with bundled applications, communications software, and its own integrated database. No system requires the small amount of care as an AS/400.

Ease of Migration

The system provides the ability to integrate new technologies with very little disruption to business operations. AS/400 users have been benefiting for many years. For instance, Pagnotti Enterprises of Wilkes-Barre, Pennsylvania, a holding company for some mining and insurance businesses, replaced its old AS/400 CISC architecture system with a 64-bit RISC system in 1999. The company's RISC machine is now old, and they are looking again. Despite the magnitude of the 1999 shift, resulting in a major performance increase, no changes were required to the application code or logic, according to Betty Carpenter, IT director for the company.

"The conversion to 64-bit was as simple as restoring the objects on the new system," said Carpenter, who has worked on AS/400s for more than a decade. That's why AS/400 customers do not want to switch.

In 1988, IBM launched the AS/400 to replace its aging System/38. Over the years, IBM has kept many of the original features but adapted the overall system to the technology changes needed for the times. Over these 38 years, counting the System/38 years, IBM also has succeeded in making the platform far more open than anyone ever would have expected. For instance, the AS/400 today offers native support for mail and messaging technologies, such as Lotus Domino and ERP, from companies such as SAP, PeopleSoft, and Baan.

The AS/400 has become a mainframe in size at the large end, and a mainframe in capability on all models. Super mainframe capability can be seen in a concept called logical partitioning on the AS/400. This feature was borrowed directly from the mainframe. Using this facility, an implementer can define one AS/400 as if it were many AS/400s, and each one can behave as a separate machine. Moreover, one AS/400 may be running OS/400, Linux, or IBM's AIX at the same time. The future is wide open. In private meetings, IBM has announced that Bill Gates would like Windows to run on an AS/400, and IBM has not ruled it out.

How Popular Is the AS/400?

Besides my little cadre of customers in Northeastern Pennsylvania, there are several hundred thousand others. Of course, I think they all should be my consulting customers, but I am happy with what I have got. A few national and world-class IBM AS/400 customers, last time I checked, include the following:

Enterprise Rent A Car,
With over 40 AS/400s, 20 of which are dedicated to handling
an application with 1.3 million transactions each hour.
Ball-Foster Glass Container Co.
In Muncie, Indiana.
J&L Fiber Service
In Waukesha, Wisconsin, a materials supplier for the paper
industry.
Cornerstone Retail Solutions
In Austin, Texas.
Bergen Brunswig Corp.,
A pharmaceutical distributor in Orange, California.
Saab Cars USA,
Inc., in Norcross, Georgia (U.S. headquarters).
AppsMall
(AppsMall.com) in Rochester, Minnesota.
CoreMark, (formerly Klein Wholesale)
In Pennsylvania, the fifth-largest candy and tobacco
wholesaler in the United States. Also significant in Canada
Marywood University,
Liberal Arts University in Scranton, Pennsylvania.

Better than half of all AS/400s are installed in countries
outside the United States.

You'd have to pry an AS/400 away from its users with the
biggest crowbar ever invented in order to create some
separation. Check out this comment from a leading AS/400
news company, NewsWire/400, of Penton Media:

> "We've been running our Web site on Domino on the
> AS/400, and we're not even running on the latest and
> greatest platform. We're running on a 50S. The beauty of
> it is, the thing never goes down. Our maintenance on it is
> almost nil. We don't do anything with it; it just runs."
>
> --Terry Bird, principal, Appsmall.com

It's not just the AS/400-biased media that pump the AS/400 from time to time. In an *InfoWorld* article on July 31, 2000, just before the rebranding of the AS/400 to the Power i, Maggie Biggs, writing for the "Enterprise Toolbox" section of *InfoWorld*'s e-magazine, noted that the industry perception of the AS/400 seemed to be changing.

In her article, Biggs discussed the changing perceptions as the AS/400 morphs into what she calls a powerful, dynamic e-business server. The article was published a few years after IBM had stuck the little "e" on the back of the AS/400, making it the AS/400e. While writing the article, as a matter of course, Ms. Biggs felt compelled to slam IBM for keeping the AS/400's capabilities a secret:

"Actually, the AS/400 has been e-business-ready for several years, but it's nice to see the marketing folks at IBM finally catching up with the platform's technological advances."

Biggs continues:

"Our experts from the Test Center and Info-World Review Board (made up of our free-lance writers) examined the newest release of the AS/400 and its operating system, OS/400, and expressed frustration at how under-marketed this platform is.

"After more than 10 years of advances and a metamorphosis into a beefy e-business server, the majority of people still view the AS/400 as a legacy platform. This is a shame because the AS/400 is a multifaceted server capable of fulfilling a myriad of business needs regardless of the size of the enterprise or the tasks that are thrown at it. And the AS/400 continues to be one of few platforms that can simultaneously support legacy, client/server, and Web-based computing.

"...what kind of ROI you might expect to gain by adopting the AS/400... found the costs low when compared to the software and hardware capabilities of the platform, which stand out favorably in many ways when measured against competing servers...

"These servers can be configured to meet the requirements and budgets of businesses both large and small. IBM has enabled technologies that let you run both Unix-based applications and Windows NT and Windows 2000 applications within your AS/400 environment. You might use these technologies to consolidate servers, reduce expenditures, or to improve business process integration...

"From what we experienced during our testing and analysis, the AS/400 appears ready to provide some stiff competition for its server rivals. You may not hear about the AS/400 as often as you might hear about other platforms, but just ask any of your colleagues who have worked with the platform and I think you'll hear a positive response."

Amen!

As the client/server revolution went sour and Windows server farms began proving to be more and more difficult and expensive to manage, despite IBM's stoicism about advertising the platform, there has recently been a definite resurgence of interest in the AS/400 server, fueled by word of mouth. Businesses seeking a reliable, scalable platform are starting to notice that out of all the technology that is inside the AS/400, the bottom line is that it works and for the most part, it does not go down.

Though not happy about IBM's AS/400 advertising, one thing that aficionados are not complaining about is the seventh generation, 64-bit architecture of the AS/400, in that it continues to benefit from Big Blue's ongoing, multi-billion-dollar investment in AS/400 technology.

Perhaps it would help if IBM knew that when and if the marketing really starts, the customer complaints would stop.

AS/400 Waiting to Be Successful

The AS/400 is poised to become the flagship for IBM once the company chooses to hoist the flag. Besides having the most elegant packaging of computer basics, its features include enterprise e-commerce applications, native support for key Web-enabling technologies, such as Web servers, Java, Lotus Domino, and IBM's WebSphere server.

Not to be outdone by the big jobs, the server also boasts support for Windows NT, Windows 2000, Windows XP, and Windows 2003 application serving.

The free operating system shipped with the machine is on duty from the moment you turn it on. The Windows process of loading the base operating system and then adding all the Windows fix packs is not necessary. The AS/400 operating system, known as Operating System/400, or OS/400, is pre-installed, and is tested for hours before shipping. As you would expect, like the Spaghetti ad, as you list features that an operating system should have, when you talk about the AS/400's operating system, you'll find yourself saying, "It's in there!"

It is amazing that with a box like the AS/400 in its stable, IBM has chosen not to let my neighbors in on the secret. In their daily lives, my neighbors, who I introduced to you in chapter 2, either operate or are retired from successful businesses. Here's a picture of Carol Anstett of John Anstett Realtors and Jeanne Elinsky of Roscoe Advertising and Noble Furniture at their party best (Figure 5-2).

Figure 5-2 Neighbors from John Anstett Real Estate, Wilkes-Barre, PA, and Noble Furniture, Nanticoke, PA -- Never Met an AS/400!

None of these fine neighbors ever met an AS/400! This must change. IBM has to figure out a way to tell ordinary citizens about its prized system.

-- End of Chapter 5
Excerpt from Whatever Happened to the IBM AS/400?

Chapter 14   A Bank President and Two Techno Geeks

From the Book: *What Happened to the IBM AS/400*
Chapter 7 Bill Gates, Steven Jobs, and Otto Robinson

AS/400 Users Love the Machine

Show me a business with a computer shop that runs the
AS/400 with a reasonably competent staff, and I'll show you
a set of very pleased IT professionals. AS/400 people love
the AS/400. It is a modern-day phenomenon. In one
independent survey after another, AS/400 users, display
more computer bias and are downright bigots regarding their
machine, compared with all others. They have very good
reason.

David H. Andrews is one of the most respected consultants in
the AS/400 marketplace. As proprietor of the D.H. Andrews
Group, he tests the attitudes of AS/400 customers
periodically. Through his consultancy, based in Cheshire,
Connecticut, over the years, Andrews has conducted
countless surveys of IBM AS/400 customers and others in
the industry. Andrews' work offers powerful insights for
customers to examine and for IBM to evaluate in making
future plans for its product set.

Ironically, in the survey mechanism and its ultimate
reporting, part of the encouragement for the customer-survey
takers to work through the survey mechanism was a caveat
that the only way that the AS/400 culture can be preserved

and extended is for IBM to get a clear message of its customers' plans for the platform.

The results of the year-2000 Andrews survey have long been available for analysis, and they reflect the same attitudes that AS/400 customers have today, and for many years. AS/400 users are arguably the truest and bluest of all IBM's customers, and are perhaps the most loyal customers in the 30-plus-year history of the midrange computer. This is not to say that the customers who are firmly lined up in the AS/400 camp are as firmly entrenched in the IBM camp. In fact, because of the way IBM is holding this group hostage today, extorting larger fees for those who choose to use an AS/400 as an AS/400, there is considerable discontent with IBM as a company within the ranks (see Chapter 24, "The Dead Goose That Once Laid Golden Eggs").

One of the least favorable conclusions that Andrews drew from the survey is that the enthusiasm which respondents show about their AS/400s, in terms of the value of the platform, is disproportional to their concerns about the level of support that IBM and its partners will put behind the AS/400 in the future.

Besides the obvious black eye, the negative for IBM is, of course, that these same AS/400 customers are increasingly looking at alternative platforms and cross-platform development technologies. Obviously, this indicates a willingness to be in a position to jump off the AS/400 platform if they feel they have to exit or find a viable alternative to the AS/400.

That said, the study concluded that the AS/400 would continue to be the primary platform for the majority of respondents for some time to come. There is no other machine that is similar to the AS/400, but the mixed results of his survey indicate a love so deep for this platform that the respondents would be pleased to take on the benefits of a similar platform from a company other than IBM.

For those of you interested in reading D.H. Andrews'
information first hand, go to
www.andrewscg-commerce.com/as400.html.

The Most Reliable System in the Industry

As noted previously, the most cited reason that AS/400 users
continue with the platform is that it is built like a brick house.
It just does not go down. It does not check out in the middle
of the night for unknown reasons, forcing a business into a
panic. It is stable; it is reliable; and it is there when you need
it. While the average PC server experiences several weeks of
down time each year, the AS/400 checks in with a measly
five hours. Most AS/400 shops claim no unplanned
downtime whatsoever.

No matter how reliable a machine may be, nobody buys
anything just because it is reliable. My pencil doesn't go
down, either, but I would not pick a pencil as the main data
processor to run my business. The reason why the AS/400
gets such high marks is that it provides high-quality business
solutions, which are more customizable than on any other
platform. AS/400s allow businesses to react to change more
rapidly than any other platform.

If you are Bill Gates, Steven Jobs, or Otto Robinson, you
chose your AS/400 because it is the only machine that can
give you the competitive edge necessary. With the AS/400,
these three people have been able to plan for change in their
industry and be leaders rather than followers in molding their
computer systems to fit the ever-changing complexion of their
businesses.

Bill Gates Used AS/400s to Run His Business

Business managers and executives typically are unconsciously unaware that their production data processing systems and decision support systems are using AS/400 technology. Perhaps the most unconscious IBM AS/400 customer of all is Bill Gates, the "barbarian leader" from Microsoft. For many years Microsoft executives slept restfully at night, knowing, according to many observers, that their business was safe because it was running on 23 silent AS/400s in a back room someplace, way out of sight. Though the evidence is no longer as obvious, the rumor mill suggests that Gates and company still process on AS/400s, but they do not take D.H. Andrews satisfaction surveys.

Steven Jobs Used AS/400s to Run His Business

Steven Jobs and Apple, many years ago, when the brilliant Jobs was alive and running Apple the first time, he decided to switch from the five DEC VAX units on which they were running their highly profitable microcomputer business, to the IBM System/38 platform. The System/38 is, of course, the direct predecessor to the AS/400.

Many industry analysts, who were familiar with both the former DEC (swallowed by Compaq, which was swallowed by HP) and IBM, give credit to IBM's AS/400 box for actually taking DEC out of the midrange computing business. The AS/400 killed the DEC VAX and made the company easy prey for the PC leader of the day, Compaq, to acquire. Now, as noted, even Compaq has disappeared from the computing scene.

When I look back at Apple's decision to move to the AS/400 product set, it is obvious that there had to be a compelling reason. At the time, Apple's major product was the Mac. As a terminal to DEC machines, the Mac worked quite well. It had a natural serial interface and terminal emulation software. DEC users could just plug a Mac into the Network, and with the proper software it would just work. The same was true for Mac users. Apple was able to place DEC servers on their Ethernet networks or serial networks, and they would connect with few technical issues.

The System/38, never in its lifetime supported serial (ASCII) terminal devices, and it never supported Ethernet or AppleTalk or any other Local Area Network protocol. In other words, the Macs could not connect to the System/38. Being a renegade company, Apple saw something in the System/38 that it did not see in any other computer in the industry.

Apple knew it would be able to react to business changes more quickly with a System/38 than any previous computer system, including the DEC boxes. It was so important for Apple to use the System/38 that the company created Rube Goldberg special devices and then jury-rigged the company with the devices to enable their Macs to talk to the System/38.

When the AS/400 came out, it had what was needed. It eventually supported both serial (ASCII) and Ethernet, as well as AppleTalk, so that the Mac became a natural device. But Apple had selected the System/38 when industry observers would have concluded that there was no way for the Mac to participate. Thus, there is no doubt that Apple Computer loves its System/38s, and now its AS/400 systems. Today, there is actually more reason for the AS/400 and the Mac to be friends. They are, in fact, relatives. The underlying technology in the new PowerMacs is a similar to the PowerPC technology that IBM uses in its AS/400 and Power i line.

The early Apple says a lot for the desirability of the System/38 and AS/400 systems as IBM products. Back in the early 1980s, Apple saw that there was a definite competitive advantage in using the box as its business system, and the company made sure that it did what was necessary to allow that to happen.

Otto Robinson Used an AS/400 to Run His Business

At Penn Security Bank in Scranton, Pennsylvania, Bank President, scientist, and entrepreneur Otto P. Robinson Jr. was told outright by IBM that the System/38 was not to be used as a modern banking computer. IBM clearly told Robinson on numerous occasions that neither the System/38 nor the AS/400 was a banking machine, and would never become a banking machine.

IBM suggested that the Penn Security Bank president look at its mainframe line of computers. IBM did not want his business if he wanted a System/38. Mr. Robinson, a very bright individual who, besides being bank president, is also a lawyer and a mathematician, was perplexed that IBM would purposely deny the banking industry the use of what he believed to be its finest computer system of the day.

Robinson was relentless in his dealings with IBM, and he never gave up. He knew the System/38 and later the AS/400 and Power I were the best computer systems in the industry, and he could not understand why IBM would deny small bankers the use of such a perfect machine.

Despite IBM's desire not to sell him one, Robinson ordered a System/38 for the bank. Because IBM had created an adapter for the magnetic ink character recognition (MICR) reader that the bank needed to process checks, his programming team converted his System/3-based batch banking software to the System/38 platform.

Meanwhile, Otto Robinson was actively lobbying IBM for banking devices (teller terminals and ATMs) to be natively supported on the System/38. I had the pleasure of being the assigned account systems engineer to Penn Security Bank, so I got to see all of this action first hand.

Robinson just would not take no for an answer. Eventually, his notoriety in doing things with the System/38 that nobody else was able to do brought him invitations to speak at COMMON and other computer and banking trade shows.

Ironically, the same IBM that had told him that he should not use a System/38 invited the outspoken bank president to various IBM-sponsored banking seminars across the country to demonstrate his effective use of the System/38. Operating without a muzzle, each time he slammed IBM for its lack of System/38 support to the banking industry and challenged IBM to get its act together.

Robinson did not sit still in his own shop, either. He discovered his own hardware solution for the terminal incompatibility. Just as Apple could not naturally connect its Macs, Otto could not connect IBM's leading-edge teller terminals. The System/38 supported just one terminal type. It was known as the IBM 5250. It was a green-screen terminal that at the time was more capable than the mainframe-oriented IBM 3270 terminal set.

Moreover, IBM did not even support its old time communication protocols on the System/38. These had very technical sounding names, such as the BISYNC telecommunications protocol or the ASYNC ASCII protocol. IBM supported its green-screen 5250s through the then new Systems Network Architecture/Synchronous Data Link Control (SNA/SDLC) protocol.

Working through all that technical mumbo jumbo, it meant that the System/38 box could not even attach the older mainframe style terminals and it could not attach the IBM's new 3600-style BISYNC banking terminals. Clearly, the System/38 had been left out of the banking picture intentionally, since this was traditional IBM mainframe territory.

Enter the Wild Ducks

Within IBM over the years, I had the pleasure of meeting and working with a number of "wild ducks." Sometimes these ducks were left alone to achieve greatness in IBM. One such duck was a talented engineer named Ed Brucklis. Brucklis worked out of IBM's Boca Raton, Florida, plant. When I met Mr. Brucklis, he had just written a program for IBM's Series/1 minicomputer that could be used to enable the attachment of unsupported terminals, such as 3270 BISYNC terminals, to the IBM System/38. In essence, Brucklis did for IBM what Apple's engineers did for Apple. Through his program, 3270 BISYNC terminals were able to talk to the IBM System/38.

Since Brucklis's Series/1 front-end creation was developed in the same Boca Raton facility that offered limited banking support to IBM's midrange customers, he was persuaded to carry his creation one step further. He added the translation for IBM 3600 Teller Terminals and ATMs. It did not take long for Otto Robinson to get word that an ATM hardware solution (through Brucklis in the Rube Goldberg vein) for the System/38 was now available. (Okay, so I told him!) Brucklis himself eventually helped make it work for the bank president.

After he realized the boxes could connect and talk, Robinson discovered an old ATM software package that had been built for the System/3 line of computers in the early 1970s. This program, written by IBM's Bill Pinkerton and others, permitted IBM's ATMs to be controlled by very old System/3 programs. Robinson worked with his local IBM systems engineer, yours truly, to research whether this package could be made to run on the System/38. I offered my endorsement and recommended how to proceed. Robinson ordered the package and some IBM ATMs, and I worked with the programming team to make sure the ATMs would light up and deliver the cash.

Before going live, Robinson once again beseeched IBM. This time, he argued for an encryption routine for the AS/400. IBM again reminded Robinson that the System/38 was not a banking machine. In frustration, Robinson ordered the BASIC language for the System/38 and wrote his own data encryption standard (DES) routine, using the BASIC programming language.

ATMs were so important to small banks around the world that Robinson opened his doors to any and all to see the marvels of the System/38 controlling a network of ATMs. From as far away as Indonesia, System/38 banking people came and were impressed, and many moved forward with their own System/38 implementations.

As nationwide ATM networks began to spring up everywhere, CashStream, Cirrhus, and Mac were the big players. Robinson contracted with CashStream, and his team then had to modify the Pinkerton ATM package even further to accept ATM cards from non-Penn Security customers. This was also a success.

System/38 Home Banking? Why Not?

In the early 1980s, banks were experimenting with some innovative notions like bill paying systems and home banking. An astute banker, Robinson saw the need to enter this marketplace. At the time, not even the big players had a presence.

Otto Robinson had no problem investing in technology. He had a super lead analyst on his IT team named Gerry Rodski, who was the best application designer in the business. Otto commissioned Mr. Rodski to design and develop his home banking software even before the bank president was sure he would be able to accept calls from his client's home banking units.

Robinson went to IBM again and asked about ASCII terminal support for what he termed videotex. IBM again reminded Robinson that the System/38 was not a banking machine and that it supported only the 5250-style terminal data stream, and there were no plans to change this.

Robinson called over his local IBM marketing team to discuss his dilemma. He did not want to know what the System/38 could not do. He was already using ATMs on the System/38, and IBM had said that he could not do that with the System/38. I had been working with Series/1s at the time, since IBM was pressuring its branch offices to sell these systems. IBM gave me the job of seeing what we could do with this most unpopular box in our local branch office.

I introduced Otto Robinson to the idea of using another Series/1 running the Yale ASCII terminal package. This package could support any type of ASCII terminal in existence, including the RCA Videotex Terminal, of which Robinson was particularly fond. The problem was that the Yale ASCII Series/1 wanted its host to speak the BISYNC 3270 data stream. It would then convert it to ASYNC ASCII, the necessary protocol. Unfortunately again, IBM's System/38 spoke only SDLC and the 5250-style data stream.

Once again, Ed Brucklis came to the rescue. It seems that the original intent of the translation software originally written by Mr. Brucklis was to permit 3270 BISYNC terminals to attach to the System/38. This was just what the Yale ASCII package wanted. So again Mr. Robinson was pushing the

IBM envelope trying to use technology that was not yet
available for the System/38.

The Rube Goldberg Home Banking Solution

Long before Internet computing, in his model home-banking
scenario, Robinson envisioned a bank customer with an RCA
Videotex terminal dialing the Yale ASCII Series/1 at the
bank. He saw the Yale ASCII Series/1 converting the
ASYNC ASCII data to BISYNC 3270 for the original
Brucklis Series/1.

The Brucklis Series/1 would then convert the BISYNC 3270
data signals into SDLC 5250 signals and send the twice-
converted data stream to the System/38. The System/38
would think it was talking to a directly attached native 5250
terminal. In reality, the connection was from a dialed-in
terminal device three systems away. (Phew! If you had a
hard time following that, there is no need to worry. You are
not alone.) Eventually it worked, but not right away.

Not knowing if this would work, IBM agreed for Ken
LeFevre, a Series/1 specialist from Philadelphia to make a
house call with yours truly on Otto Robinson. Though he
thought it was a very novel idea that may have unforeseen
issues, LeFevre could not offer any reason for this approach
not to work, and gave it his stamp of approval. Robinson
then bought his second Series/1, and in short order, in the
test environment, the System/38 was talking to dial-in RCA
devices using the two Series/1s in between. But there was a
problem.

Hang Up! Please!

Since the AS/400 had no notion of dial-in terminals, there
was no way to tell the System/38 that the dial-in banking
customer had disconnected. This created a big problem. If
another banking customer called into the same phone line,

after a prior customer had hung up, he would be connected to the same session the prior user thought he had exited. Obviously, in the banking industry especially, this compromised security. Clever as it was, it would not do the whole job.

Robinson went back to IBM, which, of course, again reminded him that the System/38 did not support banking or ASCII terminals. Otto Robinson reminded IBM that it had taken the money for the second Series/1s and the Yale ASCII package. Every now and then, the lawyer in Robinson would show his face. IBM agreed to have Ed Brucklis himself visit the bank, but did not imply that this technique would be supported or that it would ever work.

When Brucklis arrived from Boca Raton, it was snowing in Scranton, and he did not have an overcoat. Soon after Brucklis' arrival, we went to lunch about a block away from the bank. Mr. Brucklis got a taste of Scranton, Pennsylvania, winters that he would not soon forget. It was food for some gentle jabs when we sat down at Shookey's Restaurant. At lunch, there was some peppy conversation between the bank president and the software engineer. The two hit it off and formed a bond that was quite understandable. Both men would never accept the decks they were dealt, and when faced with what others would call insurmountable obstacles, they were able to devise methods to surmount them.

Robinson muses sometimes about the wild duck characteristics he saw in Ed Brucklis. They were a good team. When Brucklis saw the home banking workshop, he was obviously tickled that his work was being used so cleverly. The RCA Videotex terminals were set up using TV sets as monitors.

The Home Banking Skunk-Works Demo

Robinson demonstrated the home banking skunk-works setup and showed the problem with the dial disconnect. He asked

Brucklis how the product could possibly be usable with such a major flaw. I can still remember when Brucklis stood, undaunted, and gently fired back at Robinson: "When this product was written, nobody ever thought it would ever have to talk to a Philco TV." Both men roared with laughter, and Brucklis vowed to make it work. He did. Over time, he became one of Robinson's favorite IBMers.

When the AS/400 came out, Penn Security Bank was in line for one of the first. The bank made the transition painlessly from the System/38. When IBM announced RISC-based AS/400 models in 1995, again Penn Security was one of the first IBM customers lined up to make the transition. And, again, it was mostly painless.

Otto P. Robinson Jr. is still the bank president and still uses the AS/400 to give him the competitive edge he needs in the banking industry. Thanks to Otto Robinson and his unrelenting input to the IBM planning processes, unlike the System/38, the AS/400 is able to handle the unique requirements of banking, as well as home banking.

Who's the Fool?

Bill Gates, Steven Jobs, and Otto Robinson are not fools. What did they see in the AS/400 predecessor (System/38) that would encourage them to go through one hoop after another to be able to deploy the AS/400 heritage platform in their businesses? What makes the AS/400 so special that Microsoft, with a now less than amicable relationship with IBM, and an operating system (Windows Server) that directly competes against AS/400s, persists in its use of the platform?

They did not know or care that the AS/400 or System/38 had 48-bit or 64-bit hardware. They did not know that the system uses 128-bit software addressing. In some cases, they did not even care that it did not have the hardware support to

allow for essential devices to be attached. It was not
hardware. It was not IBM, for sure.

What they saw in the AS/400 (and the System/38) was a
machine that could help them run their businesses with
minimal issues and disruptions. More importantly, in many
ways they saw a system that would give them an edge over
their competitors so that they could adapt their business
systems to the changing times at speeds unattainable on any
other system.

Otto Robinson saw it as a survival issue. Steven Jobs saw it
as a business issue. I've got to believe that Bill Gates, like
Otto Robinson, saw it as a survival issue. He needed a
system to make his rapidly growing business survive.
Quietly, the AS/400, using OS/400, did the job for all three.

AS/400 Plusses

The time from conception to implementation has always
been far less with the AS/400 (System/38) product line.
Some developers will say 5 to 1; others as much as 10 to 1.
This ratio is the relative speed that application development
and program maintenance and updates can be performed on
the AS/400 compared with all other platforms.

For businesses wanting the competitive edge, there is no time
to wait for the important functions and features to be rolled
into the industry-standard packages. Therefore, you must
build them yourself. The AS/400 plays well in this arena.
Ask Bill Gates! Ask Steven Jobs! Ask Otto Robinson!

**-- End of Chapter 7 Excerpt from Whatever Happened to
the IBM AS/400--**

Chapter 15   Why No AS/400 Marketing?

From the Book: *What Happened to the IBM AS/400?*
Chapter 23 It's the Marketing, IBM

...

Poor AS/400 Marketing Takes Center Stage

Evans- Correia noted that Power i poor marketing took center stage again at the COMMON Conference as it has for the past six years or more that I can remember. IBM executives were pummeled with complaints about the company's poor AS/400 marketing. Al Zollar may very well get it, but he appears constrained by the same type of thinking in IBM that decided that Fort Knox was a good deal for the company.

It has become common knowledge that IBM's corporate marketing department has decided that none of its IBM-made eServers will be advertised on TV. That factoid does nothing to ameliorate the concerns of AS/400 stalwarts that IBM is not highlighting their favorite product. Additionally, if you are the head of the AS/400 division, it gives you no wiggle room when your customers are nailing you to the wall in a public meeting at COMMON.

If I were Al Zollar at COMMON's Sound-Off, I would be hoping for time to fly because there was nothing that could be said to the AS/400 crowd to make them feel like they were about to get any help from IBM. Of course, he could have lied but he's a better man than that. He had to know that AS/400 customers, whose jobs IBM's decisions affect, would be going back to AS/400 shops in which there is continual

bickering with the Windows contingent about whether the
AS/400 is worth its salt. Unfortunately, he was not able to
give them much help.

PC "gurus" are often preoccupied with dancing bears and
spinning globes, but when these arduous tasks are completed,
they find time to tell their company executives, and whoever
will listen, about how the company should be using Windows
or UNIX to run its business. IBM's public silence about the
AS/400 as a fine business server helps give the small-time PC
guy's talk much more weight in an organization than it
should have. That's why AS/400 customers at Sound-Off
hoped that IBM would change its mind and that Mr. Zollar
would be able to tell them that things were going to get better.
That message never came.

From one source or another, insiders and outsiders are
pounding IBM executives about its "legacy" AS/400.
AS/400 IT staffs are very annoyed at IBM because they have
to handle all the heat themselves.

For close to 10 years, IBM has floundered in its message and
consistently refused to advertise on TV to help its customers
fight its battle. Many AS/400 shops are concerned that they
are ultimately going to lose the war as their company makes a
decision, stupid though it may be, to switch to a more
popular non-AS/400 platform, such as Windows or Unix, or
more than likely, the current darling, Linux.

How About Some Help, Al?

Al Zollar does understand that these friends of IBM and the
AS/400 need his help. They are crying for help. He hears
them. They are telling IBM through Zollar that they need
help N-O-W. Unfortunately, at this COMMON his message
was not too consoling. After more than six years of begging
for TV advertising Mr. Zollar was forced to hem and haw
about giving AS/400 professionals what they have been and
continue to ask for. They feel they need help with their

executives through living room, emotional advertising. IBM's corporate advertising power brokers apparently have given the AS/400 division no wiggle room with advertising and that message was very clear.

Microsoft gets CEOs and the rest of us in the living room. Because of that, most regular human beings think more highly of Microsoft as a computer company than they do of IBM. By the time your company executives get to the boardroom, their decisions are often made from information that they picked up in sources such as living room advertising.

Besides, it's been a long time since IBM had a sales force able to come face to face with a real customer on the customer's premises. So, with no one-on-one and no one-on-many customer meetings -- as a marketing strategy, IBM today hooks few new AS/400 customers. Whether in the living room or in the boardroom, IBM marketing is in absentia. It doesn't get the business because it's not there asking for it.

Why Aren't IBM AS/400 Ads on TV?

Evans-Correia's perspective is that after getting the question squarely in his face, Zollar wasn't about to buckle under the pressure. He was obviously more concerned about not giving hope to the beleaguered AS/400 masses than telling them that he was not permitted to offer any. After six years of no action, Zollar tried this one on the group:

"We are not going to invest in TV until we can prove it sells."

Hey, what exactly does that mean? IBM is going to wait until it proves that by not advertising, it can find out whether advertising sells. Maybe it meant that IBM would do test marketing? No, it means that Mr. Zollar has not been given any advertising dollars and it looks like he will not be given any advertising dollars. But, he could not really say that.

It's really too bad that IBM will not advertise its "z," "p," or "i" Series machines. Surely it is that IBM strategy that makes IT major after IT major turn away from IBM's best servers. No wonder more and more companies think that IBM is not for them. One would think that if IBM is not going to tell America and the world how great its products are, few on their own will conclude that they have any merit at all.

With no choice and no relief available for the crowd, Mr. Zollar shared with the masses that he was very aware of the image the Power i has among the general populous, but he insisted that advertising the Power i on TV would not change the server's image. IBM's eServer corporate advertising contingent ruled the day.

Even if Al Zollar heard Al Barsa's famous diatribe to Tom Jarosh of four years ago, he would still have been powerless in this setting while representing IBM's corporate advertising curmudgeons. AS/400 COMMON folks may remember how Al Barsa pulled no punches as he let Tom Jarosh, Zollar's predecessor once removed, know how most of his AS/400 customers felt about IBM's advertising.

> "Every executive in the United States knows what Archer Daniels Midland does. And Archer Daniels Midland sold $12.8 billion last year, although I would bet you that 90 percent of those business executives have never done anything more on a farm than just visit. Yet AS/400 and its drag-along business is $16 billion, and no one has ever heard of it. The AS/400 absolutely needs large-scale advertising . . . the AS/400 has got to be on television."
> Al Barsa, Barsa Consulting, www.barsaconsulting.com, Article Feedback Power i News, August, 1, 1998

Zollar did his best to calm down the crowd at COMMON but he did not have the right message. In fairness to Zollar, I

don't think there was anything that he was able to do. Big
IBM again was the culprit.

While COMMON users pointed out to Zollar that they felt
that Microsoft Windows products are pushing the Power i
into oblivion, Zollar again tried to deflect the bullets. He
shared that IBM is not going to declare war on Windows. He
suggested that such a task is futile.

What I got out of that is that IBM thinks fighting Microsoft is
futile. He added that nobody is going to be able to best
Windows in terms of user base and general popularity, and
then said:

**"There's no amount of money that's going to make that
happen."**

That certainly is the IBM marketing campaign that I have
been watching since Bill Gates stole the whole PC business
from IBM. Why IBM chooses to never put up a good fight to
get it back is always a puzzle to me. If Bill Gates thought the
way IBM thinks, Microsoft Internet Explorer would never
have taken on Netscape and Windows NT Server would
never have taken on Novell. In both instances, Microsoft
was a dark horse but still chose to engage and win. The
defeatist attitude from the top of IBM surely reflects the lack
of marketing actions that AS/400 users observe and lament.
Al Zollar may be perceived as part of the AS/400 problem,
but sending an unarmed man to fight Microsoft is not Al's
fault; it's IBM's. The company just doesn't get it.

This IBM message would be the last thing I would want to
deliver at a COMMON Conference. It might have helped Al
Zollar to be transparent but he was bigger than that. Maybe
with the May 4, 2000 announcements the AS/400 will get a
little boost and maybe the IBM corporate advertising team
will have a new mission or maybe they will be replaced.

Folks who know Mr. Zollar have shared with me that he is a good guy and that because of him; functions like WebSphere will be able to be integrated into the new I5 server. If the AS/400 becomes stronger, perhaps Al Zollar will be in a better position to bring advertising gifts or stories the next time he gets to visit COMMON.

Can you imagine Bill Gates taking IBM on and winning, and now IBM's AS/400 general manager is put in a position in which he must pay homage to the corporate advertising masters by suggesting that taking on Bill Gates' little company would be futile? "Nobody is going to be able to best Windows." That's great, IBM. So what does IBM do now? Roll over?

IBM sure thinks it knows best. In the next part of the discussion, Mr. Zollar noted that it "is not an intergalactic battle!"

The fact is that the IBM / Microsoft foray is not a battle at all because IBM corporate does not permit the company to fight. As always, when facing Bill Gates, Big Blue is unarmed and waving a white flag. This time, IBM had all the guns locked up. Winding up his session, Mr. Zollar then requested input from the group as he asked:

> **"Are there as many people buying Power i as Windows? No. But that doesn't mean [the Power i] is not going to be successful."**

As you can see, he answered his own question. Zollar's arguments, summed up, mean that AS/400 customers should not expect advertising from IBM because IBM thinks the AS/400 is as successful as it wants it to be at this point of its life.

Unfortunately, IBM gave Mr. Zollar no rope in being able to help the AS/400 customer set with IBM's AS/400 market perception problem. Doing that for the COMMON crowd was clearly beyond his granted powers. Suggesting the AS/400 is going to be successful under all circumstances was the best he was able to do.

I don't mean to be disrespectful to Al Zollar, or to anybody in IBM, but like most AS/400 loyalists, I am very annoyed. Every day I am one of those people asking for IBM to listen so that the AS/400 can survive.

Even when I was with the company, IBM would claim that it has empowered all of its employees to do their jobs effectively. From my eyes, IBM has set up the AS/400 GM job with inadequate power. The AS/400 GM cannot make the AS/400 successful since he is not empowered (budget-wise) to do so. That sums up IBM's COMMON experience. Hopefully, IBM will do better next time and the time after.

An AS/400 Marketing Department

Eventually at the COMMON conference, a lady with a sense of humor from the IBM team came to speak. Cecelia Maresse is vice president of Power i marketing. She also tried to defuse the agitated crowd by noting that IBM planned to look deeper into the TV market but needed to take its time testing the waters, promoting the eServer brand itself, before the Power i in particular.

I know that the IBM executives at COMMON were all bright but they had an impossible mission -- trying to defend its marketing. Until I knew what Cecelia Maresse's title was, I did not think that IBM had a marketing department for the Power i worthy of a vice presidential slot. Again, that is not a personal shot at Ms. Maresse. I see no IBM marketing that helps the product in a meaningful way.

After noting that IBM had to take its time with the company-specific server ads, Maresse expanded her statements:

> **"We're just starting our television advertising…for now, we have no Power i plans. We're going to see what this [current TV ads] tells us."**

Maresse, like Al Zollar, is just doing her job. But it sure would be nice to find somebody who has the power to make a real decision in IBM. Maresse's words, though honestly spoken, did not warm me up at all, and they offered little consolation to the crowd at COMMON. In my mind, I kept hearing the words of Paul Simon:

> **"Cecelia, you're breaking my heart.**
> **You're shaking my confidence daily.**
> **Oh, Cecelia, I'm down on my knees.**
> **I'm begging you please to go home."**

You might as well go back to Rochester, because you do not have the power or the budget to help. The eServer has been out for four years or so now, and I have been watching the silly eServer ads for that long, wondering when I was going to hear the word Power i. Not once! The ads are not working for the Power i; that is for sure, because there are none!

I sometimes have bad dreams about waking in a cold sweat and finding myself in a very embarrassing, un-winnable situation. I transferred my dream fear to the plight of Maresse at COMMON. How would you like to be on the panel of a meeting in which the theme is, "It's the marketing, IBM," and you look down at your name tag and you notice that you hold the title *Vice President for Power i Marketing.* Wow!

Though not permitted to bear gifts of advertising from her superiors, Maresse injected a little humorous reality for the crowd when she related getting zapped herself by IBM's refusal to highlight the Power i on TV. Evidently she had

shared with her children that she worked with the big bad
Power i computer.

Watching TV at home the weekend before COMMON, she
felt defeat from the minds of a miniature crew of attackers,
her own children. During one of the IBM ad segments that
previous weekend, her two children, ages 13 and 11, saw an
eServer homogenization piece and asked their mom,
"Where's the Power i?" Hey, Cecelia, it's the marketing.

At the fall 2003 COMMON session, it was nice that the
AS/400 constituency had an opportunity to talk to the
honchos and get their information directly from the horses'
mouths. It's too bad that the output message of the session
seemed to come from the other direction. One could only
conclude that IBM's executives were not empowered to help.

At COMMON, 2003 IBM Rochester via Mr. Zollar and Ms.
Maresse got the message clearly again from its customers. It
is the marketing, IBM!

Will they do anything? In all fairness to both, neither
probably has enough corporate power to change much about
what is bothering their customers. But I do get the sense they
would like to – and that's good.

What a Difference a Day Makes!

I had the opportunity to update this ending after IBM's May
4, 2004 grand Power5 announcements. While I was
rethinking my ending, Al Zollar and Cecelia Maresse were
back at COMMON's Spring Conference.

I am very pleased to say that Mr. Zollar brought a number of
gifts with him to the "Soundoff Town Hall Meeting" at
COMMON. My friends tell me that Zollar was beaming
with the news he offered, and rightfully so.

Mr. Zollar introduced the new I5 machines and the new pricing and the new IBM impetus for winning the business. He would not let his superiors send him to COMMON unarmed this time. Moreover, Ms. Maresse and Mr. Zollar silenced the crowd when they announced that IBM was getting ready to advertise the Power i on TV.

Unlike COMMON 2003, IBM had armed its executives with a full chest of gifts. Nobody dared say, "It's the Marketing, IBM." At least not on this day.

-- End of Chapter 23 Excerpt from Whatever Happened to the IBM AS/400?

Chapter 16   Are All IBM Systems the Same?

From the Book: *What Happened to the IBM AS/400?*
Chapter 24 Homogenization Shows No Cream

I'm Nobody, Who Are You?

Randall Munson would probably describe himself in these inimitable words of Emily Dickinson: "I'm nobody, who are you?"

Yet Randall Munson is somebody. In 2003, for the umpteenth time, he walked away from a COMMON conference with a gold medal designating him a speaker of excellence. This award is one given to a very elite group. Typically two to four speakers get the gold at COMMON's semi-annual AS/400 technical conference. Munson is so good, he is always on the list.

He is a former IBMer, who for part of his 20 years, worked in the Rochester AS/400 labs in operating system development. That means that Munson cannot only talk well, he can also program and design software, as proven by his role in the architecture of OS/400 (IBM i). I had the pleasure of attending a number of Munson's award winning technical presentations over the years. I have firsthand knowledge of the power in his speech and the knowledge that he puts forth when he speaks about AS/400 technical topics and personal development topics.

In early September 2003, Maryann Ratchford, a staff reporter from Power i News interviewed Munson, and the results of that interview were mailed to AS/400 supporters all over the

world. I received my own copy. In this interview, the
reporter asks a stirring question to Munson, the answer to
which in many ways is part of the underlying theme of this
book. The question and the answer are shown below:

Interview of Randall Munson by Power i News acquisitions
editor MaryAnn Ratchford:

> **News/400 Reporter: If you could take Sam Palmisano's
> place for a day, would you do anything differently with
> regard to the Power i [AS/400]?**
>
> **Munson: IBM has intentionally restructured the branding
> for all of their platforms. They've devoted a lot of
> resources and a lot of work in doing that to make them
> appear very homogenous.**
>
> **What's unfortunate for the Power i [AS/400] is that it's a
> very unique platform, and when these platforms are all
> melded together, the uniqueness, the quality, is not
> coming out. Things like the Power i / IBM I architecture
> and its intrinsic power for database and business
> intelligence; the inherent security of the architecture as
> opposed to other systems that are constantly being hit with
> viruses, hacking, and so forth; the unparalleled reliability
> of the system -- these are being downplayed because, in
> contrast, they make the other servers look bad.**
>
> **So, if I were in his position, although I certainly would
> keep the eServer branding intact, I would take advantage
> of those unique attributes of the iSeries –Power i [AS/400]
> that could be used to my benefit in the marketplace.**

IBM has intentionally taken its product lines and thrown
them into a big stew, and the individual flavors are becoming
indiscernible. Munson's description of homogenization is
right on.

With homogenization, the cream does not rise to the top. So
if the AS/400 is part of a bigger soup called eServer, that
means that it must taste like the rest of the broth and forget
about adding a special zing or two that would help the guy
with the spoon know that the last chunk swallowed was from
the AS/400 stock.

No, in a homogenization strategy, everything is supposed to look and taste the same. In a homogenization marketing strategy, everything is advertised as being the same. So in order to be hosted as part of the eServer advertising stew, the AS/400 had to promise to leave its uniqueness at home and provide only sameness to the brew.

Those of us out here in real world know that nobody buys an eServer. You actually cannot buy the soup that is being sold. You can only buy chunks that you can find in the advertising broth.

But how does a potential consumer become aware of what chunks are in the stew? That's a good question. The answer, of course, is most damaging to the AS/400. The consumer never finds out. Hey, it's a stew!

So how do they find the other chunks? Working from the bottom of the server line up, the Windows folks have Intel and Microsoft advertising their wares. If somebody happens to be interested in IBM eServer homogenized stew, Microsoft and Intel give them enough information to spot their chunks in the eServer stew. They can have IBM or a systems integrator give them a quote. However, I can't see anybody buying an IBM PC-based server by studying the eServer ads.

At the next level of server, there are the Unix geeks, who want Unix operating system facility no matter what. Again, if these folks are inclined to want that kind of capability in an IBM product, they already know enough to spot the Unix and the Linux chunks in the IBM eServer stew.

They can then ask IBM to give them information using a tear-away from an eServer ad, or they can ask an IBM Unix/Linux integrator or business partner (if they can find one) to give them a quote on a Unix/Linux chunk of the eServer homogenized stew.

Well, that means that two out of the four ingredients can be sold separately, even though they are part of the same advertising stew. Their loyal followers will come calling. No more or no less will come calling than would have if IBM did not advertise, but, nonetheless, they will come looking for their Unix/Linux chunks, and their Wintel chunks, and when those chunks are sold, the leftover eServer stew will contain just IBM's proprietary systems, mainframes, and AS/400s.

-- End of Chapter 24 Excerpt from Whatever Happened to the IBM AS/400—

Chapter 17   IBM Changes Are Not Good!

From the Book: *What Happened to the IBM AS/400?*
Chapter 30 It's No Longer Watson's IBM

Nothing Great Lasts Forever

There is no doubt that there is a new IBM today, compared with the IBM that Thomas Watson Sr. forged almost 100 years ago. Though its roots spring back to the 1890s, the 20th century IBM began in 1915, when Thomas J. Watson Sr. became its president after 11 months as general manager.

A Watson ran the IBM that we know from then until T. Vincent Learson took over a year after Thomas Watson Jr. suffered a heart attack. Learson was a great friend of Watson, and his brief 18-month stint was more of a continuation of a Watson than the dawning of a new era.

However, when Frank Cary became chairman, in 1973, IBM did enter a new era. The company had been aggressive in the same fashion as Microsoft's early years. There was no such thing as an unimportant sale, and there was no such thing as a good competitor. Thomas Watson Sr. was the consummate manager and marketer, while Watson Jr. was much more Gates-ish, and he took some enormous risks for the ultimate benefit of the company.

When the Watsons disappeared, IBM became less agile, more sluggish and less sure and less capable of moving or sustaining a marketing battle. Besides not being as business savvy or entrepreneurial, once the Watson's were gone, the new IBM's notion of people orientation was more of a paper thing than a real thing.

Wild Ducks Are Welcome

Tom Watson Sr. had set IBM up as a company that cared about its people and their families. Watson Jr. carried on that tradition. My most favorite Watson story has to do with Thomas J. Jr.'s notion of wild ducks.

In his book *A Business and Its Beliefs: The Ideas That Helped Build IBM* (McGraw Hill, 1963), Thomas Watson Jr. described his business philosophies. Among these was the notion that if you take care of the people, the people will take care of the business. Watson meant it.

He was known and loved by mostly all employees during his term with IBM. He was especially fond of people who today we would say, "Think out of the box." Watson called them "wild ducks," and did his best to preserve the notion of wild ducks in his time with IBM. In his book, he writes:

> "In IBM, we frequently refer to our need for 'wild ducks.' The moral is drawn from a story by the Danish philosopher Soren Kierkegaard. He told of a man on the coast of New Zealand who liked to watch the wild ducks fly south in great flocks each fall. "Out of charity, he took to putting feed for them in a nearby pond. After a while, some of the ducks no longer bothered to fly south; they wintered in Denmark on what he fed them.

> "In time, they flew less and less. When the wild ducks returned, the others would circle up to greet them but then head back to their feeding grounds on the pond. After three or four years, they grew so lazy and fat that they found difficulty in flying at all

> "Kierkegaard drew his point--you can make wild ducks tame, but you can never make tame ducks wild again. One might also add that the duck, who is tamed will never go anywhere any more.

> "We are convinced that any business needs its wild ducks. And, in IBM, we try not to tame them."

The Irreplaceable Thomas J. Watson Jr.

On the wall in my sunroom, since 1994, I have had a page from the January 5, 1994, *Wall Street Journal* pinned up. It was cut out and hand delivered to me by my good friend and neighbor John Anstett. After a few years as a Christmas gift, my adult children had it framed for me.

Lou Gerstner's IBM remembered Thomas Watson Jr. with a magnificent tribute, a full page memorial to the wonderful man and great corporate leader, Thomas Watson Jr. My sunroom continues to be graced with this picture of the IBM person that I admire the most, though I never met him. The IBM tribute to Thomas J. Watson Jr. was as good as anything that was ever said about anybody. Thank you, IBM, for your caring and thoughtfulness in this regard: Under his picture, the tribute reads as follows:

"For all his achievements –
as a visionary, entrepreneur, corporate leader
and distinguished statesman, --
we will remember Thomas J. Watson, Jr. most
for his adventurous spirit,
his innate sense of fair play,
and the vigor of his friendship.
We mourn his passing
but we will be forever grateful that he lived".

[*Wall Street Journal*, Wed. Jan. 5, 1994, Final Tribute to TJ Watson Jr., 1914 to 1993] Picture from Wall Street Journal shown in Figure 30-1

Figure 30-1 Thomas J. Watson Jr.'s Picture in IBM's Final Tribute

Thomas J. Watson, Jr.
1914-1993

I loved the Watson-era IBM. I felt good working for the Watson IBM. Though starched white shirts were the order of the day at IBM in those days--and I wore mine with delight--there was tremendous pride and caring for every employee. And every employee knew the train of care did not stop until it reached the very top. Watson's IBM! That's the IBM I joined. I still miss those days.

That was the old IBM. The new IBM took a while to take effect. Though we may speculate that it was from Frank Cary, 1973 onward, the new IBM appeared for all to see in the very early 1990s. It could no longer be hidden from public scrutiny. Seemingly, from out of nowhere, little things started to happen in the company that showed that all ducks, both wild and tame, were no longer as important to IBM. None were safe from the new IBM's employee axe.

The first signs were quite innocuous. For example, for years, IBM deposited my paycheck or gave me a check several days before the pay period ended. I can recall telling my dad about that when I was first hired. He thought that it was wonderful. I thought it was wonderful.

At the brewery where he worked, he had to wait until the Thursday after to get his weekly paycheck. Then, one day, in the 1980s, without announcement, my paycheck arrived right on time and not a minute earlier. It was that way from then on. It was not a big deal. But it signified a big change.

One another day in the late 1980s, IBM announced that it was concerned about the cost of healthcare as it affected the company. At the time, no employee contributed for healthcare in any way, and retirees' healthcare was just as good. IBM announced that it would pay no more than a specified amount for healthcare forever. It would never again be adjusted for inflation.

It was unprecedented, but it was representative of the new IBM. Because of this change, more and more of the cost of healthcare began to be borne by employees and retirees. Before joining Medicare, after being retired for four years, the cost of my part of IBM healthcare had gone up to $18,000. It was as if I had no pension

For some retirees, healthcare has eaten up a lot more than half of their retirement income. Some specifics about IBM's change regarding healthcare are included at the end of this chapter.

The new IBM seemed not to have time or money to care about unimportant things like employee or retiree well-being as long as the accounting was good and it favored the company. For some this may not be a big deal, but for IBMers who had trusted IBM with sixteen-hour days waiting for their day in the sun, it is a very big deal, and it signified a new hardened and impersonal IBM.

It is the kind of IBM of which even IBMers are no longer proud. It's sure not a Watson-like IBM. Though the new IBM "caretakers" undoubtedly feel that they pulled one over on the employees and former employees by substantially reducing their expectations, these new IBM executives will leave behind a legacy that was unknown to the Watsons. It will be one with few kind words written about them.

...

-- End of Chapter 30 Excerpt from Whatever Happened to the IBM AS/400--

Chapter 18   How to Make IBM a Better Company

From the Book: *What Happened to the IBM AS/400?*
Chapter 32 Suggestions for Improvement

What Can IBM Do?

At this point in the book, it is no secret that IBM's biggest AS/400 problem is that it fails to market the machine. The company has restructured its business as a services and software supplier, and that is at the heart of its problem. Hardware, including the AS/400 does not count for much anymore. Some of us think that a little care and feeding and marketing could have and could still help that. If you take a trip to IBM's main Web site, www.ibm.com, it is difficult to find anything about its hardware products, but there sure is a lot about solutions. Though solutions may include hardware, the primary ingredients are software and tailoring services.

"Solutions" is a euphemism for the things that IBM thinks customers buy when they are shopping for a computer system. IBM thinks it sells solutions in today's world. As strange as it may be, the IBM Company does not sell application solutions software. It is purposely not in that marketplace. It is not in that business. So, why would solutions be important?

IBM sells hardware, middleware, and services. The company has a dotted line relationship to its independent Business Partners and it depends on their good will as to whether IBM hardware is included in their partners' software solutions.

IBM would like to think that its Business Partners propose its products and only its products; however, this is not the case. I have been in a number of sales situations where these "loyal;" AS/400 solutions providers will gladly switch to a Unix or Windows solution if the customer balks at the price of an AS/400. They say "it is the same software, why not run it on the least expensive machine." The moral is that just like the Computerland stores of yesteryear, IBM's Business Partners are not in business for IBM's benefit; they do not sell just IBM; and they are quite **independent.**

IBM loves to sell all kinds of services, as you would see from a trip to its Web site. Since most of IBM's business is services and software, the company has apparently decided that hardware is now in the drag-along category. Years ago, IBM would sell hardware as a solution. Software products and services were the drag-along business. Now it is completely the opposite.

Though IBM still makes about $30 billion in hardware, until this year, the number has been dropping. Right now, its $30 billion hardware business is still integral to the company's success. But, in the long term, as services and software revenues climb, hardware will have less and less of an impact.

The hardware business has become less important to IBM and the company simply has not been successful in maintaining its hardware revenue or market share. In many ways the reason for its decreased sales is because hardware is just not an area in which the new IBM pays attention. In fact, IBM seems to be selling off all of its hardware divisions lately.

In late 2003, IBM announced that its software division would focus its solutions on vertical marketplaces as opposed to selling software to whomever will buy it. Since the vertical strategy is already employed in Rochester, this is not expected to affect the AS/400. However, I think that it will.

When a lumber company comes to IBM for its one stop shopping, IBM's Software Division will direct them to a software package for the industry as well as try to ensure that some of what is on the IBM software truck is sold. Since the AS/400 software truck is not as full as the other trucks, and since its most important AS/400 middleware comes with the machine, human nature says that if the software division has a prospect, it is going to sell what it's got on its truck. Since they get less compensation for an AS/400 sale, the AS/400 will not be sold. Case closed.

Therefore, you can bet none of these companies who contact the software division will ever hear about the AS/400 -- other than perhaps an acknowledgment that it is more expensive than Unix and Windows.

The Grim Reaper

They say that in life you reap what you sew. Unless IBM re-acknowledges that it is in the hardware businesses before it fritters its server business away, just as it did the PC business, the AS/400 and its hardware sisters and stepmother will be gone before the company knows it. When that happens, the discussion about how to save the AS/400 will be moot.

Though some may argue with me about it, the best thing that can happen to the IBM AS/400 is for Microsoft to buy the whole business from IBM or for IBM to donate OS/400 to the Open Source Foundation. There would be no question that Bill Gates would highlight the product if it were his and he'd win the small and large server business by killing both Unix and the mainframe.

Eventually, he'd put a GUI on the AS/400 and would drive the box with Windows-like icons. In addition to making AS/400 customers happy this would make Microsoft happy

also. Microsoft's internal IT staff would not have to be
embarrassed anymore about running (or having run) the
business on the AS/400 platform. Besides peace internally,
Bill Gates would finally have a highly scalable and reliable
platform upon which to run Windows. Intel need not apply.
Don't rule it out!

A donation to the open source community would help IBM
in a number of ways. AS/400 customers would get off IBM's
back because the software would be open and free. IBM
would not have to bear the cost of maintaining OS/400. The
Open Source OS/400 may be tweaked to run on many
different hardware platforms, including all of IBM's servers.

Short of action from Microsoft, or the donation route, if IBM
chooses to save its AS/400 product line, this chapter has a
number of suggestions. It starts with the top nine things the
company can do and then generally discusses the problems
that some of the nine solutions would address.

The suggestion list continues in the Chapter titled *Teach Me!
Teach Me! Teach Me!* with another set of suggestions for how
to attract new blood to the AS/400 and how to get them
prepared for training. If IBM is ready to sell, sell, sell, there
is no doubt that the AS/400 can be saved.

To the IBM Vault?

What can IBM do to prevent the AS/400 from finding its
way into the IBM vault? Vestiges from IBM's glorious and
ignominious past are displayed in the vault. For example,
you'll find the Series/1, the 305 RAMAC, the DataMaster,
the 8100, the 1620, the DisplayWriter, and the Ford Edsel?
Ford has its Edsel there because it did not have a vault and
Disney would not take it.

Unlike the Disney vault, the IBM vault has an entrance but
no exit. Products that go to the vault don't ever get taken out

for a new look – even after the kids that worked with them have grown up. The list of suggestions to IBM then is intended to help keep the AS/400 from getting tossed into the vault along with the dead products of yesteryear.

In one form or another I would suppose that others have given these recommendations to IBM over the last ten years, but perhaps not all together as the list below and the education list in Chapter 34.

When I read this list I say to myself, "of course, that will save the AS/400...yes, that's a good one, etc." But I am powerless and you are powerless other than to suggest. Suggestions or no suggestions, in the end it is IBM who must decide to what level its AS/400 has a role in its company. Based on the IBM view, the AS/400 may hit the vault or not.

AS/400 Partial Improvement List

1. Tell the world about AS/400 reliability and dependability. Since most AS/400 users believe that the most important part of an AS/400 is its reliability and dependability, IBM should tell somebody about it. Marketing is not about best kept secrets

2. Tell the world about the marvels of AS/400 integration. Since IBM thinks that the most important part of the AS/400 is its integration characteristics (as in **Power i**), again, tell somebody about it, and begin to integrate the many standalone products, such as WebSphere to keep the "i" in Power i from meaning "dis **i** ntegrated.".

3. Position the AS/400 as a new account business computer. Since no business expands without some new accounts, and new accounts don't come calling by themselves, again, IBM should tell somebody that they want new accounts and that they can sustain new accounts. A new accounts S.W.A.T. team would help in this regard.

4. Create a new baby sized AS/400 server / personal machine. Since the PowerPC chip line is so dominant in non-PC circles (almost all chips in game toys are IBM's), the company should use this chip to create an AS/400 style machine to sell to new accounts. There is really no reason to import OS/400 to the Intel platform if this is done.

Again, if IBM were to build it, the company would have to tell somebody about its new affordable AS/400 server and development machine. The machine should be sold as an integrated, affordable package at about $2,000.00 or less.

5. Give AS/400s away to students and to colleges. IBM should have a lottery once a week, on a different campus every week, in which they give away one or two small AS/400s to a college student and the host college. To qualify for the lottery, a student might be asked to bid a dollar and all the dollars would go to the institution or to Student Government.

If IBM were to create this inexpensive AS/400 I would recommend giving at least one to every college and community college as a good will gesture during its kickoff period. Of course, the company would also be compelled to tell the colleges why the AS/400 should have value to them. To do this, again, IBM would have to let somebody know about the system, as in all other scenarios. Additionally, the company would have to let the general public know that these little AS/400 boxes are coming to a college close to home so the public has the opportunity to learn about the alive and well AS/400.7

6. Add a standard GUI to the AS/400 operating system box (MAC OS). Since the AS/400 looks just like the tired old legacy system that Microsoft and the trade press have it painted to be, IBM should buy the Mac GUI from Apple and adapt it as the GUI for the AS/400. The MAC and the AS/400 both use PowerPC processor technology. Academia would automatically like the AS/400 since they love the Mac. By the way, the Mac and the Apple PowerBook use the same family of chips as the AS/400. Again, IBM would have to tell somebody about this.

An alternative would be to rebuild the OS/400 front end to use an HTML or better yet, an XML driven GUI. The AS/400 command structure could also be rescued to participate in the resolution of the commands.

7. Create a hybrid futuristic Mac/AS/400 PC. Along with Apple, IBM should build a PC that has the outward look and feel of a Mac and the inner elegance and full application facilities of an AS/400. If IBM were to perform this magic, it would create another PC revolution. To ensure success, Apple would have to market the device.

8. Take advice from Mark Twain and announce that the AS/400 is not dead and that it is not even tired. Since no business wants to install a server or even upgrade one that is dead, and the trade press has declared that the AS/400 and green screens are dead, and IBM behaves as if the AS/400 actually is dead, the company, like Mark Twain should announce that the

AS/400 is not dead and that the reports of its death have been greatly exaggerated. Again, IBM must tell someone about this.

9. Add generic aliases to the IBM server line, making the AS/400 the "IBM Business System." Rather than have IBM embarrass itself by discarding the eServer umbrella, add a generic primary differentiator name to the eServer brand so that the system can be known by a generic alias. Generic aliases for the other systems are already unofficially in place -- IBM Mainframe Server; IBM Unix Server; IBM PC (x86) Server. The IBM Business System or even the IBM Business Server moniker would properly position the AS/400 and clear up its primary purpose.

10. etc. The list continues.

The Absence of AS/400 Awareness

In order to offer suggestions for improvement, you must examine the problems that the AS/400 platform is currently experiencing that makes it an at-risk-system in the 21st century. Most of my peers with whom I communicate share the thought that IBM's biggest problem with its AS/400 line of computers, besides IBM per se, is buyer awareness. Other than the AS/400 professionals, the IT folks who manage, develop, implement, and operate AS/400 systems on a regular basis, there is almost no awareness of the product. There is even less awareness of its new pseudonym, *Power i.*

Interestingly, this is not much different than the early days of computing when only the insiders knew what an IBM 1130, a System/3, or a System/38 might be like. In the early days, very few people knew anything about any computer, other than those people working directly with computers in their businesses. That is not the case today.

More people know about computers today than those who do not know about them. More importantly, ordinary people know computers today from things they do and see outside of their workplace. Just like the days gone by, not many people, other than those directly involved, know anything about the big back room computers that do the companies work every day.

Who are the people then who know little about their computer at work but are very aware of computers in the rest of their lives? You already know who they are. They are my neighbors and they are your neighbors. Four out of five of them are likely to have at least one computer at home and nineteen out of twenty are likely to have a close relative with one.

This same percentage of people is on the Internet every day or so, looking for an email from a son or daughter or parent or other loved one, or perhaps an acknowledgment that their last big purchase, such as a digital camera, CD, or cell phone has been shipped.

These people are Firemen, Accountants, Nurses, Police, Food Service Workers, Maintenance Personnel, Doctors, Plumbers, CEOs, Store Owners, Sales People, Secretaries, Street Cleaners, Teachers, Linemen, Clergy, Cable Workers, Bankers, other government workers, other school workers, and other industry workers.

Please don't forget the retirees, because many of us continue to persevere in the job marketplace. Of course we can't forget the computer geeks and the students from high school to college to graduate school. All of these people, you and I included; know much more about computers in our home lives than people ever did before.

Opinion's Count

Because we see computers in our own homes and in the homes of our friends, you and I are more likely to have formed some opinions about computers. For example, because your Windows computer locks up frequently and you lose information from time to time and you have to re-key things, you may have concluded that is a normal behavior for a computer. By the way, it is not. Because of your opinion, however, you might be inclined to think that computers that are reliable are nowhere to be found. That too is not true. Because you may run out of space in your database on your C drive and you watch your system crash, you may have already gone through a scenario that forces you to move some files to the D drive. Because of your poor experience, you may think that all computers are like that. Again, that is not the case. Theoretically, if you never got the real answers above, your opinions might stand, unchecked by reality.

Moreover, because we have all heard the names Intel and Microsoft in our homes and in our neighbors' homes, and since we know that they make most of the computers in the world, you may think that all businesses either do or should use these very popular computers.

You may not be consciously thinking about this, but if you thought about it, you may have these types of opinions from your own experience with computers. Again, this is not true but it is the normal conclusion that one would make from being in the world of today.

The point is that you have gained an opinion of computers over time because of who you are and where you go, etc. Companies named Microsoft and Intel are part of your world, like it or not. It is probably safe to say that, as a rule, unless you happen to have an IBM PC or a friend has an IBM PC (less than 5% of the market), you don't even associate IBM with the kind of computers that normal human beings use in the course of their off work hours activities.

You may think that big companies and big government and big medical facilities might use IBM computers, but more than likely, you and others like you have not bumped into any of these behemoths in your personal life.

TV Advertising Delivers the Best Message

While you and I and the rest of the listed people above, my neighbors and your neighbors are sitting at home resting, perhaps watching a TV program or a game, or listening to music on the radio, companies of all sorts are permitted into our leisure time to give us an advertising message of some kind or another that we probably would rather not hear. Somehow, with no effort expended on our part, we learn that Chevy is like a rock, and that the models at Victoria's secret are not what are for sale, and that beef is what's for dinner. Like it or not, they get us.

IBM is the exception. The IBM Company does not take the time to reach us at home very often, so we know little about IBM and what IBM is all about. Moreover, IBM's messages are always cryptic so we never know what they are selling. This is a major fault of IBM's since most of the general public knows little about IBM.

Therefore, why would any one of us look to IBM for a computer for our business? Microsoft and Apple and Intel, on the other hand are lots smarter than IBM. They have some great ads that help us know they are out there and they encourage us to buy their products. It follows that if IBM were to show up with a competing offer to one of these three without having spent the effort acquainting us with IBM products, you and I and the general public would be more inclined to go with one of the three.

It stands to reason that there would be an affinity with the companies that we have heard about, rather than a company that has never ever cared to tell us anything about how its products can help our businesses.

The ads from Microsoft and Apple and others that I show in the next section are very good. I present them here because IBM can and should do the same type of thing to enhance its product and company images. Have you ever seen this ad?

Our mission is not just to unlock the potential of today's new technologies. It is to help unleash the potential in every person, family, and business. We want to help you do the things you do every day-express your ideas, manage your finances, build your business-faster, easier, and better. At Microsoft, we see the world not as it is, but as it might someday become.

How about this one?

"We stand in awe of kids and their potential. We see them as doctors, as heroes, as inventors. We see their potential and make software that helps them unlock it."

How about this ad?

I'm writing to share a tragic little story.

My Dad has a PC that my sister and I used to use for our homework assignments. One night, I was writing a paper on it, when all of a sudden it went berserk, the screen started flashing, and the whole paper just disappeared. All of it. And it was a good paper! I had to cram and rewrite it really quickly. Needless to say, my rushed paper wasn't nearly as good, and I blame that PC for the grade I got.

I'm happy to report that my sister and I now share an Apple PowerBook. It's a lot nicer to work on than my dad's PC was, it hasn't let me down once, and my grades have all been really good.

Thanks, Apple.

Microsoft and Apple

Microsoft sells operating systems and personal productivity ware, such as word processing. It is safe to say that, almost everybody knows this as fact, at some level or another. Moreover, though the courts waffle sometimes about making a definite statement, Microsoft has been declared a monopoly. On the other hand, Apple is just a feisty little company taking shots at the giant every so often. You've just got to love Apple for its spunk.

In the Microsoft ads above, Microsoft is not advertising a product. They don't have to. You already know what they make. They have enough product ads in your face to tell you about their new products. When you see their Windows 2003 server ad, however, you know that they are advertising a product. You don't have to guess what they are doing as in an IBM ad. That's because they want you to go out and buy the new version of the product and they are telling you it's great, it's available, and it will save you money.

In the last ad, which is from Apple, it is clearly targeting Windows client users. The product they are selling is the Apple Power Book and the ad does a good job of letting you know what they are trying to sell. The implication is that Apple is better than Microsoft, yet they don't mention Microsoft per se, but Microsoft knows that when a PC goes down, they get the blame.

Intel gets a pass on a lock, though its processors may also cause a lock problem. That's interesting. Intel does not market to the general public and everybody, including IBM lets them get away with saying that Intel Inside means something good.

Of the three companies noted, Apple, Intel, and Microsoft, all three know what they are doing with their advertising dollars. Their ads are effective and clear and you know what product or group of products they want you to buy. If you have ever seen an IBM ad, you would not feel the same. Thus, IBM has some learning to do in this regard.

To add a little humor to this analysis, the Apple ad actually ticked off Microsoft something fierce. The big bullies at Microsoft could not let it go so they struck back with an ad of their own on their Web site. They did not take it to TV media because it did not go over too well on the Web. The ad was titled:

Confessions of a Mac to PC Convert

The ad purports to be a first-person account of a writer who decided to switch from an Apple Macintosh computer to a PC running Windows XP. It goes a little like this:

> **"Yes, it's true; I like the Microsoft Windows XP operating system enough to change my whole computing world around...Windows XP gives me more choices and flexibility and better compatibility with the rest of the computing world."**

Microsoft copied the Apple ad style of having a real person do the ad, but then the media snoops discovered that it was not a real person. The company had commissioned the "ad" from a freelance writer who was paid for her work, although Microsoft claims her experience was as reported. Microsoft also had crow for a second course as it had to admit that the "convert" shown was really not the person who they were highlighting. It was a stock photograph.

Unlike what I would expect from IBM, Microsoft admitted that it was beaten, pulled the ad in less than a week's time when they knew that they had not gotten away with it, dusted itself off, and went after the next opportunity. The company called the ad, made by Microsoft's software marketing group, "a mistake in judgment." The company then went through the customary, "regrets the action" routine and then praised itself for removing the page. Apple declined to comment on the Microsoft snub.

What Would IBM Have Done?

First of all, IBM does not have any wild ducks any more who would consider taking on any company so the whole situation could never happen. However, if IBM approved a marketing slam-dunk on Microsoft or any other company and it was met with any negatives whatsoever, the IBM thought police would be called in to argue with the objector.

Since IBM knows what is best for IBM, the company would meet the mere suggestion that something was done improperly, with strong denials. IBM would expect that all those objecting to IBM approved thought would eventually submit. Of course, Big Blue is finding that AS/400 loyalists are as tenacious against the company's position as a bulldog on a pant leg.

I happened to see an eServer ad myself a few days ago. I almost missed it. It was the first that I had ever seen. True to form, I did not know what IBM was trying to sell. The term xSeries did appear at the end of the ad at a time when I was hoping it was not a Power i ad because it was a poor excuse for advertising. As good as the Microsoft ads, the bold Apple onslaught, and the terrific Intel Inside campaign are, the IBM eServer ads do not compare. .

No Guts, No Glory

Unlike Microsoft and Apple, from my eyes, IBM has no guts. The IBM ducks fly no more, surely to Thomas Watson Jr.'s eternal lament. Unlike Intel, with its "Intel Inside" catch phrase, IBM has no marketing creativity. When I went to the Web to find sample Apple and Microsoft ads, they were all over the place, including their Web sites. When I looked for IBM ads, neither Dogpile nor Google gave me anything other than IBM's peace and love campaign for Linux with the eServer pSeries.

Considering that Linux is not an IBM product, that's odd. Even when I surfed the IBM site itself, www.ibm.com, the company kept its ad text for all campaigns a secret. It's like they knew I was coming and they hid it all. That's how little there was about IBM and advertising. There is no apparent IBM anxiety to offer any commentary on IBM's hardware products.

Peace and Love and Linux

A funny thing happened to IBM's Linux peace and love ad party. They had hired artists to cover San Francisco's sidewalks with chalked and painted symbols for its Peace and Love and Linux eServer advertising campaign. It was a good idea. City officials, however, who obviously were not consulted, viewed IBM's artwork as more graffiti to endure and when the biodegradable material did not degrade after rainstorms; the city was looking for IBM to clean up its mess. Ironically, IBM's one eServer campaign that was noticed became a PR nightmare.

And, true to form, IBM stumbled and wondered what to do. Then almost immediately, the company was faced with another potential PR nightmare because it did not act fast enough to solve this minor dilemma. Taking advantage of a situation, Sun Microsystems, IBM's ardent competitor in the Unix space, decided that it was time to act.

Sun did its best to turn this IBM marketing gaff into a public relations coup for itself. The company announced in the middle of IBM's woes that it would rescue the City of San Francisco from IBM's graffiti and it volunteered to clean up the sidewalks that Big Blue had spray-painted.

It is heartening to find marketing departments that are still sharp and opportunistic and ready to strike at a moment's notice. It is clear that IBM does not hire people like that anymore or it tames its modern ducks to meld better with its stodgy corporate culture. While IBM was taking ten years to study the matter, Sun acted. Kudos to Sun.

IBM Can Learn From Intel

When Intel is not highlighting its company name, it has no problem telling you about how special its Pentium brand is.

Unlike IBM with real end user products, nobody can actually buy an Intel. They can buy Dell and HP and Gateway, which happen to have Intel and Pentiums Inside, but they can't buy Intel brand PCs. Intel does not sell PCs. Moreover, when Intel advertises, they reach people (including CEOs) in their living rooms, not in the boardrooms. By the time the CEOs get to their boardrooms, they have a fairly positive feeling about any product that has Intel inside. And, in fact, they are probably inclined to make sure that Intel is inside, rather than take a chance on something they have never heard of.

IBM believes that it does not have to advertise its server products to regular people in their living room, though Intel finds it very effective. For about ten years IBM has promised to step up its product awareness campaign for the AS/400. The company in effect has misled its AS/400 customers on this point. That's a pretty big sin.

Al Zollar, the one-time head of the AS/400 Unit, as his excuse, said he wanted to see if advertising works. That's why IBM gets beat all of the time. IBM thinks that it must prove universal truths such as "advertising sells products." Intel just goes ahead and advertises to the public and it sets its own message rather than having it set on the street. Its customers are tickled about that and it keeps them buying Intel.

IBM acts as though its customers are wrong when they ask the company to provide some advertising support to help them prove to their management that their company made a good decision. IBM can learn a lot from Intel.

A Few Test Ads for IBM—Free of Charge

If you and I can come up with ideas as to how IBM can promote its systems, then IBM and its high paid Madison Avenue cohorts also ought to be able to do so. Here are a few neat ad ideas for the living room TV. They come from the Average Joe ad hoc department. How about a big 128-bit lion or tiger or cougar or panther with a big tongue like the Budweiser frogs, talking about its next 32-bit meal?

IBM must win the computer battle in the living room. How about an ad campaign that shows an AS/400 professional discussing the merits of the '400 with a Windows oriented computer neophyte, with the oratory -- features and functions list, in understandable terms, building to a crescendo until finally, the Windows guy says:

> **"Hey, you don't have to go any further; I want one of those. It's great! I even want one in my home."**

The AS/400 professional says:

> **"I'm sorry, the AS/400 is "industrial strength." It's made to support the mission critical needs of the world. You can't get an AS/400 for your home. It's not a home computer."**

The Windows guy laments:

> **"But I want one...."**

Wouldn't it be nice to have the Windows community lamenting that it can't get an AS/400?

> **"You can't get an AS/400 for your home. It's not a home computer,"** maybe someday?

> **"Industrial Strength computing at its best -- the AS/400."**

> **"The AS/400 is industrial strength"**

> It should be the IS/400: It's *industrial strength.*

Can "industrial strength" be the catch phrase IBM has been looking for to immediately differentiate an AS/400 from the home market units? You can buy a "blippety" dishwasher, or you can buy Maytag, which has traditionally been viewed as industrial strength. Even those that can't afford a Maytag dishwasher want one.

"Even those who think they can't afford an AS/400, still want one... but maybe you really can afford one."

The IBM Repairman Ad

How about an ad with the AS/400 computer repairman sitting in a lonely office in the same fashion as the Maytag repair man? Picture the camera moving back and the AS/400 repair office is in the middle of a repair complex, flanked by two big repair centers for PCs and PC Servers. Repairperson after repairperson are leaving the side door and coming back for more parts and bringing little PC carcasses in with them. PC users are bringing broken PC after PC through the front doors. The camera closes in on one of the repair centers and you hear... "I hope you have a backup... I understand it's your business on there but you still have to re-boot. The machine got confused"

Then the big voice of somebody such as James Earl Jones comes on and you hear:

"If you want to have your computer available for your business when you need it, choose the Industrial Strength computer -- the IS/400 (AS/400). Let your competition use a PC solution."

This can be followed by a group of PC users coming from the repair center with big oversized repair tickets instead of PCs, looking up to the sky and crying

"We want one! How do we get an AS/400?"

Eventually, people would know that an AS/400 is reliable and it is desirable.

The Living Room CEO

You don't have to be technical to understand this. But the computer mindshare battle - no matter what size computer --

must be fought in the living room. The living room CEO becomes the boardroom CEO again every Monday morning. They are one and the same people. People can be taught the meaning of PC, Unix, Mainframe and AS/400 in simple terms by IBM ads if IBM chooses to fight. IBM, you got that? "In the living room!" And down the road, maybe IBM can actually set the stage for something that gets IBM machines back on the desktop.

-- End of Chapter 32 Excerpt from Whatever Happened to the IBM AS/400--

Chapter 19   More and Better IBM Improvements

From the Book: *What Happened to the IBM AS/400?*
Chapter 34 Teach Me! Teach Me! Teach Me!

How Could IBM Help in Higher Education If It Chose To Help?

In many ways, the things that IBM could and should do for the AS/400 are things that occur naturally to help the Windows server platform. If IBM were inclined to sell new AS/400 accounts and spread the word about the AS/400 and make it easy for people to learn, there are a few things that Big Blue could work on to help make the AS/400 a desirable system to learn. Though there is some overlap with the recommended improvement list in the chapter titled: *Suggestions for Improvement*, these recommendations pertain to the "training issue" per se if there really is one. A non-prioritized, numbered list follows:

1. Introduce a mini AS/400 for one-person businesses and for the home.

There are hundreds of millions of PCs across the world. Ninety nine percent of all PCs are Windows PCs. The rest are Linux. You may know that Linus Torvalds invented Linux because DOS / Windows was such a sloppy operating system and Unix was too expensive. A PC-based AS/400 would help expand mindshare, which is the biggest detriment to AS/400 style computing.

2. Hire a SWAT team of good-will ambassadors who can give short seminars at local colleges, universities, and town halls.

Use this team to conduct one-day AS/400 seminars at least twice a year in all areas of the world and invite all the business people. Run half-day public seminars (town hall meetings) for anybody wanting to come.

3. Stop treating AS/400 education classes as a profit-oriented business.

Education should be bundled with system sales so that one or several people can be trained for free.

4. Provide a free, AS/400 self-learning center over the Internet.

Using this center, IBM customers or anybody wanting to know, can come and be assured that a person will be there for questions, using a form of Chat to answer questions within a reasonable period.

5. Sponsor public debates on Educational TV.

All factions, Windows, Linux, and AS/400, should be presented and debated.

6. Create AS/400 memorabilia and a fun-to-watch demo CD.

Attractive cartoon-like, give-away AS/400 dolls could be commissioned to give the platform a friendly face. A well-done "AS/400 as a business system" CD or DVD could also spark some interest.

7. Start a "you, too, can know the AS/400 campaign" for kids.

Bring back Captain IBM and Captain 400 to tag team the kids at their schools or after school. Meet them on their turf in grade school, high school, and college, and tell them what the AS/400 is all about. Invite the press to special events

8. Encourage former systems engineers and marketing reps and former Rochester people to help educate the masses on the AS/400.

IBM treats folks like me more as competitors than as hands willing to help. Maybe some ex IBMers, such as me, would volunteer their time. IBM has never asked its ex-employees with AS/400 expertise for anything, including the time of day. At any rate, IBM can take advantage of their former employees' willingness to help by treating them with some dignity.

Note: When IBM dismantled its field force, thousands of local IBM Systems Engineers went off into the sunset. This was a potential army of loyal AS/400 types. At the time, local management was happy just to get rid of their employ, never to see them again. In retrospect, this intelligent herd could have been unleashed with a positive message to IBM customers. IBM could have also helped systems engineer's keep abreast of the system to be in a position to help customers. This is still a good idea.

In my particular case, IBM was so paranoid that they viewed my helping my clients as competing with the local office. In my first summer, I received a notice from corporate counsel. I construed this to mean cease and desist. One of my former peers had turned me in for helping my clients, who were AS/400 shops, and may also have been IBM's services clients.

The local office then insisted that I get approval for every engagement or seminar that I was to run just in case that they decided to do the same thing. It wasn't nice and it certainly did not help IBM's AS/400 customers. IBM went so far as to send an IBMer to teach a seminar onsite at one of my clients, after I had asked permission, rather than permit me to gain the business. IBM never charged for this particular seminar.

9. Conduct a wake-up, one-time, three-month marketing blitz from IBM branch office sites or hotels close by the former site.

Bring back as many former IBM marketing reps. systems engineers, and former local managers as part-time temporary employees to conduct such blitzes. A person working for IBM should visit every customer and prospect (especially K-12 schools and colleges) at least once during this period, offering special deals on systems bought under the program.

AS/400 Memorabilia and the CD/DVD that demonstrates powerful AS/400 features should be provided. Free AS/400 education should be available at the IBM Branch Office or a rented site for the entire blitz period. The visit to all IBM customers and non-customers can help them know that IBM is in town and the AS/400 really is not dead.

For added support, a direct mail campaign to local businesses should precede the blitz along with all the details of what customers and prospects should expect from the visit. Figure out how to make the Business Partners help by paying them for sales made during the program.

10. Change the name of the AS/400 or Power System for IBM I or the Power i (whatever it may be called) from its current name to *The IBM Business System* with no numbers. If this change is made, the two tag team captains could be captain IBM and captain IBS. Change the name of the RPG programming language to the Business Language and make it available on all platforms.

Just a Start

These are just a few ideas to help generate a demand for training and to get some training accomplished. If IBM decides to market the AS/400, I'm sure the marketing experts at IBM would add many more items to this list. Until then! It surely would help IBM to achieve #1 again to get started on the list. Make it a 10 to 15 year rollout with a roadmap.

Chapter 20   A Look at John Opel's Years with IBM

From the Book: *Thank You IBM*
Chapter 44. John Opel—CEO with Spirit, Opportunity, Failure

Opel was not Watson-trained

Let's immediately begin this John Opel part by discussing IBM and its killer PC. It was brought into the marketplace during John Opel's tenure at IBM. IBM was not in the PC business when John Opel took the reins from Frank T. Cary

IBM only became the recognized leader in PC technology when it finally introduced its groundbreaking PC. This occurred in the first year of John Opel's tenure as Chairman but the effort behind it came from the work of former Chair, Frank Cary.

Before the IBM PC was announced few analysts thought that there would be anything wrong with a mainframe oriented computer company introducing a small hobby, home or personal computers and not making a big push to dominate this new area of endeavor. In other words, it would be OK for Big Blue to try its hand at becoming an also-ran in toy sized computer units.

And, so, the PC marketplace in which IBM found itself in the late 1970's and into 1980 and 1981 was not something the executives in the board room planned to conquer. IBM did what was expected and was content to be an also-ran in

the diminutive home computer and hobby marketplace.
Hey, it was a passing fad anyway? Right?

It had become embarrassing for IBM Executives in public
speaking engagements that the largest computer company in
the world could not create a computer system that would
operate at the home and personal level. IBM executives read
the papers and answered questions from their grandkids
about what grandpop really did for a living. Did he really
help Santa Claus? And why could Santa not bring a PC with
IBM's name on it?

IBM Executives were making enough money. They simply
wanted to save face at home. Their efforts to produce a unit
to compete in the personal space, were the boldest steps ever
for an IBM that most often waited five to ten years from
idea to product. But, then again, this product was more like
company advertising than something real? It was just a
placeholder to protect IBM as a company that could make
anything. It was not to be taken seriously by the IT industry.

To repeat, few industry analysts at the time thought that Big
Blue's board of directors had big intentions of the Company
becoming the champion in the home computer marketplace.
Just a few geeks were using home computers at the time
though the learning games for kids were getting much better.
This was not real bad thinking at the time. Before the IBM
PC was announced there was apparently no real big, billion
dollar type marketplace envisioned for IBM to capture.
Could IBM have really missed a trillion dollar market? They
sure did!

With little risk, IBM therefore came out with its PC mostly
to prove to the masses that it was a real computer company.
As folklore has it, it was OK to not try hard with the PC
because IBM did not need the business. It was announced
simply because IBM executives were sick of being
embarrassed at home when their grandchildren asked why

their PC said Apple, Radio Shack, TI or Atari. Why were there no computers at home made by grandpop's company?

Mostly everybody in the first sixth of the 21st century has a perspective on PCs because they are so dominant today in our lives. For example, according to IDC, over 300 million PC's were sold in 2014, and another 3 million larger pc servers (x86 servers) were sold during the same period. Somebody made a lot of money on those units, and nobody is thanking IBM for their largesse in giving the business to other companies but they should be for sure.

If all this business were IBM's, at $1000 per desktop/laptop unit, the revenue would be $300 billion, and if we suggest that PC (i86) servers go for $10,000, then we would add another $25 billion to the mix. Can you believe that with just PCs, IBM would be a $325 billion company when with its current repertoire of products and services, the Company is less than $100 billion and revenue is decreasing each year. Something has been wrong in Denmark for IBM for some time.

And, of course we are not counting the chipmakers, tablet makers, phone makers, game consoles, etc. all of which were spawned from the acceptance of the IBM PC. If we had a calculator with enough digits, we would find the total value of the PC marketplace over is at least $500 billion and more likely a $trillion dollars in revenue or even more each year. For IBM, it was a big market to lose and today to be left without even a trace of business in this lucrative profit area, is unimaginable.

Before we move into the introduction of IBM's PC during the Opel years, we need to take a look at what the notion of home computing was all about in the 1970's. Since all of this pre-PC activity was begun during the Frank T. Cary regime at IBM, the microcomputer revolution is chronicled in

Section III, which you just absorbed. Feel free to read that section again to get the proper perspective.

The computerists of this 1970's pre-PC era would be known as geeks today. Perhaps that is how they saw themselves back then. They were tinkerers and thinkers with big brains and their minds were focused on technology for the sake of technology, and because it was cool! IBM employees may have been in their ranks but until 1981, the IBM Company was not in the marketplace.

IBM ignored Apple in the beginning as the IBM Company seemed to have had nine million Wozniak's working in its zillion labs across the world. It continued to ignore Apple when the PC was the big winner in the marketplace but the Apple II and its derivatives continued to sell big time, and Apple had a following of people, most of whom did not like IBM, Intel or Microsoft.

What IBM never had was a guy like Steven Jobs, who could turn a piece of dirt into success, if he chose to do so. He had that much positive energy as a CEO and as a tech leader. It is well rumored that the IBM Board thought about correcting IBM's stodgy version of success when the Company was ready to replace John Akers for the Chairmanship. Akers of course resigned as was required for IBM to succeed.

Jobs was more than a contender for IBM's CEO position. Unfortunately for IBM, Jobs stuck with his mettle and he and his rejuvenated Apple killed IBM in the marketplace. IBM today and its stockholders wish it could be Apple. Apple revenue is 2X IBM today. Apple will never have to say thank you IBM as it won victory over IBM by its own capabilities, not by IBM's weaknesses. I admit that the gains may not have been as great if IBM were paying attention to business.

Apple people never got a special gift of instant insider as Bill Gates' people did. Thank you John Opel. In the Microsoft chapter, please note how Bill Gates mother asked John Opel for a favor, and IBM has been paying for that favor ever since.

IBM had no idea that the Home Computer would actually produce a marketplace and if they thought it would, they would never have believed that a big computer company like IBM should ever try to be involved.

As an example of IBM's mainframe myopia, neither CEO Frank Cary nor his successor, John R. Opel would bring a RISC based minicomputer product to the marketplace during their respective tenures. Cary served until Opel's appointment as CEO in 1981. Both resisted making IBM's General Systems Division mainstream even though its technology outclassed the mainframe IBMers in Poughkeepsie.

IBM was so confident, it thought it was supply constrained

Opel, as many CEO's before him, was fully absorbed by IBM's tremendous mainframe success at the time and he believed that if manufacturing constraints were lifted, IBM would move from a $50 billion company to a $100 billion company magically by 1990. Under Opel IBM made a lot of hard hats happy, spending the corporate reserves on major construction projects to increase plant space. The Company was continually building new plants and adding on to existing facilities to help make the Chairman's dream of having $100 billion in manufacturing capability by 1990 a reality.

Ironically, IBM CEOs of the past, especially in the Watson years, set up the Company so that IBM subcontractors took most of the risk of expansion along with the Company and they supplied many of the components needed for manufacturing IBM's finest systems. Why did Opel's IBM think it had to make everything? I still do not know that answer as it was not the IBM way.

Opel was not as cautious as other IBM CEOs but he had no apparent substance for his chutzpah. IBM used up way too much of its substantial cash reserves building Opel's dream factories. Then, there was so little planning for the product line that there were no major products needing to be built in the new huge facility space. IBM had failed to create a marketplace for its new manufacturing capability. What products were on the horizon that needed such space— none!

Chairman Opel's push for $100 Billion was viewed by industry insiders as pure hubris. He set IBM back almost to the stone age financially and the 50-year old John Akers expected ten year term as CEO (until he hit 60 years of age) hardly had a chance. Opel had almost burned the Company down to the ground. Unfortunately, when Akers took over, he could not smell any smoke at all and simply continued the Opel plan.

Ironically, few of the loyal soldiers such as myself understood the damage that Opel had done while it was occurring. We thought everything was la! la! la! When Akers took over and life was no longer good for IBM employees, Akers got the blame. For ex IBMers, it took a while for many of us to see it rightly. We had blamed Akers; but it was Opel.

Peter E. Greulich, of MBI Concepts Corporation, wrote an excellent article titled: "IBM's One Hundred Year History Is about Cash, Culture and Mutualism."

http://seekingalpha.com/article/2933406-ibms-one-hundred-year-history-is-about-cash-culture-and-mutualism

I would recommend this article, written by a 30-year IBMer for those looking for more. It is excellent. Here are the first three paragraphs of his article. These succinctly explain what happened in the Opel years and the influence Opel's dynasty had on John Akers prematurely giving up the Company reins to Lou Gerstner. Here it is:

"When John F. Akers assumed control of IBM, he inherited from his predecessor - John R. Opel - a market expectation that could never be met. Opel had promised a $100 billion IBM by 1990, and a $180 billion corporation by 1994. When Business Week published an article on February 18, 1985 (IBM: More Worlds to Conquer) about his goals, it used the word "hubris." It was.

"As many IBMers of the time - but few of today's analysts - remember, IBM set this expectation by playing its first corporate financial game. Most of the Company's revenue at the time came from its leased hardware install base, which it converted to a purchase model over a few short years at a fraction of its true value. In a fire sale, the Company exchanged a perennial, one-dollar gold piece for a devalued, one-time, two-dollar paper note. IBM's revenue growth was temporarily hyper-inflated to make futuristic predictions look attainable; but IBM was also financially hyper-extended.

"John Akers, in 1985, found himself in the middle of an investment and employment tsunami. He stopped the investing and hiring, and started reducing and redeploying the IBM workforce, but then he was blindsided by the 10th largest stock market decline in history. Even though IBM grew revenue by more than 50% over the next six years, we missed Opel's 1990 revenue target of $100 billion by $30 billion; and in the ensuing three years, IBM would lose $15 billion."

IBM PC came during Opel years

On the brighter side, John Opel's appointment coincided with the introduction of the IBM PC. I do remember it well. I happened to be in Boca Raton Florida, the plant of manufacture for the IBM PC. I was there for an IBM System/38 banking class. Hoping to one day be a writer, I had just purchased an $1800 memory typewriter using my employee discount. At the time, we had just one child so the cost did not really bother me.

Meanwhile, IBM still was not running at a revenue pace that would meet or eclipse John Opel's prediction that by 1990, the Company would no longer be supply constrained and IBM would therefore reach the magic $100 billion plateau. From that vantage point in the Opel plan, IBM would dominate the industry.

Instead, in my observations, IBM was lucky to have survived its many mistakes. IBM stockholders should never thank the IBM Company for the poor performance of the stock while Big Blue gave up one opportunity after another. Yet, somehow IBM has never suffered a stockholders' revolt.

What happened during the Opel years changed IBM?

It started in the Opel years but continued into the Akers years. I worked for the marketing division which ran the IBM branch offices. The IBM Company began to look at salesman and field support personnel, who put together customer solutions that could be purchased from IBM, as a drag on expenses. My buddy Dennis Grimes' father when he got wind of what IBM was doing suggested that only a company that no longer wanted to sell anything would get rid of its sales force.

The new IBM, without the marketing oriented Watsons and their good students: Learson and Cary; did not understand the value of its field marketing and engineering force. For years they had abused it and then abused it more. For proof of this, we need only check the facts. Rather than fix an administrative and computer order processing problem, IBM sacrificed its technical field force to the order processing god.

By the time the Company believed it could not afford its expensive technical field force, IBM had already contorted these highly trained technicians into an army of technical order takers. When IBM pulled the plug on technical support to its customers, there were few customers who missed it. It had been MIA for years. IBM had morphed its best systems engineers into people that its administrators could rely on to apply the right sales codes on an order so the plant would ship a new box with the stuff the customer actually ordered. Another company would have automated such a function and kept its engineers servicing customers.

What Brainiac would stop renting machines?

Thomas Watson Jr. almost brought IBM to bankruptcy as he spent $4 billion of the Company's cash reserves, and borrowed another $1 billion in order to build a new computer which in 1964, he dreamed would work, In 1981, John Opel had no clue what products he would be able to sell for IBM to meet his lofty $100 billion sales target for 1990, but he was building the plants just in case.

Frank Cary had begun to sell equipment outright in order to make earnings look a little better. John Opel needed all the sales from the rental inventory so that he could pay for all the plant capacity and human resources he was bringing on to satisfy his $100 billion dream.

Since IBM was spending its extra development dollars trying to bolster its mainframe capabilities, one would surmise that the Company had projected that its stagnant mainframe sales would begin to grow at the pace of the industry or better. Other than the mainframe investments, there was little tangible evidence that the $50 billion IBM Company at the time had any real plans as to how it was going to double in size in less than ten years.

Though they were planning to build mainframes which nobody in the whole world wanted, IBM kept building and building and building manufacturing floor space so that it could meet the demand for the products necessary to meet the Chair's 100 billion dollar projection. Millions of square feet of manufacturing space never saw an IBM product or IBM part in any stage of production. Yet, to finance all of this construction, the Company needed many billions of dollars. The Chairman would not have it any other way.

IBM "willed" that the plants be successful. Perhaps there were even corporate incantations. But there was no plan! Unfortunately, the correct product mix was never offered and the plants, as they were completed, had to be discarded and sold for pennies on the dollar. In addition to plant capacity for the unknown products, to fully assure such growth, the Company had to ramp up its headcount by over 100,000 new employees.

Nobody could increase its staff by 33%, and its plant capacity by 50% without a tremendous amount of cash. How would it be paid? Perhaps nobody even asked. After all, this was IBM. The Company managers displayed wanton disregard for the assets of the corporation as they pursued an expansion program that was not product oriented, and not crisply forecasted.

IBM's almost assured demise, would have been trumpeted by its competitors. Perhaps it was God that sent Tom Watson Jr. to meet Lou Gerstner Jr. at the airport on his first day of work. Watson was not unaware of IBM's troubles. He told the magician that IBM could not continue without good management and he made sure Gerstner knew that he expected a lot from the first CEO hire from outside of the IBM culture. That was a good ten years after Opel was banking on the impossible.

Not planning product demand for the excess capacity was a big mistake. IBM's biggest squander however, was ramping up for its big $100 billion a year achievement without financing plans. It was like the Federal Government raiding the Social Security Fund. IBM had one thing which no other business had, which was big enough that it would come close to financing the whole project.

What do you think that might be? Well remember at that time, other than a bright future in PCs, IBM rented or leased almost all of its heavy iron. John Opel could sell off IBM's rental base and compromise the future of the IBM Company to satisfy his $100 billion plant capacity bet by 1990? But, would a sane person actually do that? Opel would not only do that; he did it, and that is why Akers tenure was so tough! There was no money left for anything.

If you wanted your job in IBM at the time, it was not even a consideration to take on the Chairman about how asinine his goals were. Telling him that his financing plan was even more ludicrous was out of the question. As an IBMer at the time, hoping the executives would give us a few good plays to execute, I recall hoping somebody, who had a brain, was doing all this to the Company knowing would all work out. It just wasn't so.

The value to IBM of its rental base.

When clients rented machines from IBM, the Company's service personnel were at the ready keeping the installed gear in ship shape and fully operational at all times. When they needed more powerful equipment, much more often than not, IBM's loyal rental customers would go back to IBM and for just a few extra bucks a month, they would install their upgrade. That was the hook that IBM had with its rental customers. They were always ready to buy from IBM the next time. Growing the business was easy as there was already an income base year after year. Technically, if IBM sold nothing in a given year, its income would be the same as the prior year based on steady rentals.

With a deep rental base, IBM did not have to be that much better as long as the gear was being rented. Once the customer took title to the gear, the BUNCH, or DEC, or HP, or DG could make a sales call and with sales schmooze, convince the customer much more easily to drop IBM and get their next modern system from them rather than from IBM. Big Blue had always seen its rental business as an annuity as it was. It was an annuity that grew as the customer's business grew. John Opel did not care.

As an IBM systems engineer working with IBM customers every day, I could not believe that IBM would get rid of such a source of eternal profits—its rental base. The IBM Company unfortunately was being run by a guy who was like a cash addict. He needed a lot of revenue to pay for his building projects. John Opel chose to sell off IBM's rental base of computers... the base which literally assured IBM, year in and year out, of sustained large profits.

IBM senior executives at Opel's direction decided to move IBM from this nice, safe, steady rental business into the risky, dog-eat-dog business of selling computer products outright. There would be no steady income coming to IBM forevermore.

In some of the years during the 1980's, especially 1985, which was a peak year for revenue and profits, IBM looked like an unbeatable industry winner. It looked like senior executives had made a great decision. Unfortunately, the more rental equipment that was sold off, the more difficult it became for the Company to attain the next year's revenue objectives. Each year, more and more outright purchases needed to be achieved as less rental inventory was available for sale, and a diminished number of rented units contributed to each year's results.

Here is how bad it got. As a systems engineer, I got to read the sales commission plans for the office and the marketing managers kept us on alert for things that helped our office achieve objectives and which helped the Branch get into the 100% club.

One year in particular, certain pieces of equipment were placed on what appeared to me to be a fire sale. The customers using the gear were not about to discontinue their leases or cancel their rental options that year. However, IBM was so hard pressed for immediate cash that they offered big incentives for salesmen to bring in a check for the purchase of any existing rental machine.

I can recall that the sales pitch for the customer was easy to make. It was a great deal for customers but a poor deal for IBM. The breakeven in many cases for the customer was more often than not, less than a year, and often as little as nine months. In this case, the customer wrote a check and owned the box and never had to write another rental check.

If they wrote a check in say February for a nine month break-even machine, IBM cashed the check and "made a killing" that month. But, even a fool knew that in

November, after the breakeven date, IBM no longer would receive any rental income and thus the revenue for the year for that piece of equipment was less than if the client had continued renting the machine.

Year after year, IBM sold off more and more of its success base. By the 1990s, only 12% of IBM's revenue came from rentals. Thus, 88% of the revenues in any given year had to come from services or be recreated from new sales. This was a formidable task for any marketing organization. Not only were few innovative product designs coming for the millions of new square feet of manufacturing space, but there was less and less of a guaranteed revenue base upon which to build.

Thus, IBM's growth slowed to a standstill, and actually began to decline in the 1990s. When there was just about no rental base left, and coincidentally the world slipped into a hard recession, IBM had no fallback plan with which to absorb the shock of such a major decrease in sales. Not only did IBM not reach $100 billion by 1990 (They were about $60 billion) but the Company was in such bad shape when Chairman Akers finally stepped down, the Company came close to bankruptcy.

Because he truly rescued IBM from its own demise, Lou Gerstner will more than likely one day make the business hall of fame. But, IBM, for squandering its lucrative, repeatable, rental business for the sake of creating plants for unplanned products, gets very low marks. This was one big mistake that IBM made from which no one particular competitor benefited. But, a weakened IBM, the biggest computer vendor in the world, helped all computer vendors move against IBM with impunity. IBM had no muscle to fight back. Thank you, IBM!

The revenue was there... IBM just didn't get it!

Though the Company did not achieve Opel's growth forecast of $100 billion by 1990, it was not because the number was unachievable. If we examine the success of startup firms in industries which IBM should have controlled, there was plenty of opportunity for the IBM Company to have reached its goals. Unfortunately, the Company not only planned its efforts poorly, but it suffered tremendous implementation failings. Companies with little resources, but plenty of ideas, beat IBM in market after market.

Despite being beaten by microcomputer vendors and Unix vendors, rather than taking on the challenge with a winning strategy, the Company stubbornly stayed with its mainframe emphasis. Consequently even companies never before hear of beat Big Blue regularly on many new fronts.

When we discuss this failing in this book we note that IBM got beat by everybody from microcomputer vendors to PC vendors to software vendors such as Microsoft. A large part of this major loss occurred during the Opel years. However, the selling off of the rental base made earnings look great.

With IBM today as a $92.7 billion dollar company, knowing that it once reached and surpassed $107 billion—just five years ago—IBM's big mistakes during the Opel years appear even more damaging.

IBM began the PC revolution by introducing the IBM Personal Computer during Opel's tenure. At the time, there were no real competitors so IBM management policies created all of its problems. IBM itself brought on its competition. Neither Microsoft nor Intel, IBM's biggest PC predators, needed to be in the picture at all. Microsoft revenue in 2015 exceeded IBM's for the first time. This shows how damaging it was for IBM to turn its operating system business over to Bill Gates in 1981. If Microsoft were not in the picture, that revenue would be IBM's and there never would have been any clones. Not even one clone!

IBM had the whole PC industry to itself if it moved smartly. It did not. Analysts estimate the whole PC industry brings in between a $half trillion and a $trillion each year. One would think that every IBM CEO at the time and every senior manager, especially those in forecasting, would have been fired for missing out on all that revenue. Yet, IBM's Board of Directors sat idly by as if we had not hired them to protect stockholder assets.

As noted, predecessor CEO Frank Cary had put the PC group together to make it all happen but Opel was the guy who was in charge when IBM had to sell it and make it work for its customers and for IBM. Opel did neither. He blew it big time and worse than that, he could never tell a real IBM partner from a thief.

How bad did he blow it? Opel forecast 275,000 PC units to be sold in the PC's first five years. So, with all his unneeded plant capacity on the drawing boards, the CEO did not reserve any manufacturing space in case the PC was a bit more successful than mainframe IBM had expected. On the very first day of the announcement cycle, ComputerLand, a small computer retailer ordered 250,000 units of IBM's new PC. On day one, they gobbled up almost the entire five-year forecast. What did they know that Opel did not? IBM's forecast was already way off and just one order had come in and just one day had gone by.

Final thoughts on John Opel

Though Opel was a tyrant in terms of assuring that his unrealistic goals were met; he was a gentleman also and was well liked by most IBMers. Additionally, his numbers at

IBM were phenomenal. His gift to his successor, John Akers was a company in which everything had gone negative and was not about to come back. Opel bequeathed a company in unstable condition despite its great record from the great asset selloff during the Opel years.

John R. Opel, therefore is remembered by most as the person who presided over IBM in its final period of dominance in the information-processing industry. He is also the man who oversaw the Company's move into personal computers. Though he did not cause the problem, John Akers took the rap for having destroyed IBM. Of course, Akers surely could have done a better job even with the hand he was dealt.

Things changed almost immediately after Opel left office. In the late 1980s, and early 1990's, with Akers at the helm, IBM went through a painful period of cutbacks as the computer business underwent huge changes. Small computers based on microprocessors and using standardized software increasingly took over from centralized machines using proprietary hardware and software.

Some blame IBM itself for helping bring on the shift when it introduced its first personal computer in 1981 under Opel's charge. They are correct because IBM did not see what it had actually created until the barn door was wide open and the Company had given away almost all of its assets,

The initial issue as seen in Mr. Opel's and Mr. Cary's legacy is that IBM did not design any part of the PC itself. Worse than that, it did not select its piece parts from the existing stable of IBM processors and operating systems available within the Company.

In an effort to make an inexpensive machine that could get to market quickly, it used a microprocessor from Intel and operating system software from Microsoft. IBM did nothing to protect its product from copycats. In fact, it gave away too much control of its PC project to Microsoft and Intel.

The machine was a huge hit. Thus IBM made desktop computing acceptable to corporate America and the IBM PC became the industry standard. Because IBM gave Intel all the rights to the heart of their new product, and Microsoft all the rights to the product's brains. IBM was left with nothing. Even when it should have realized the value of the operating system and micro-processor, it did nothing to stop the erosion of its product line.

In essence, competitors quickly realized they could essentially make copies of the machine using Intel chips and Microsoft software. IBM actually told Microsoft it was OK for them to market the same OS under their name for clones. IBM could not have done this without Opel's permission.

The power in the computer industry shifted to Intel and Microsoft, and hardware became a low-price commodity. IBM eventually sold its PC business because it did not know how to run this business and refused to learn. Now, of course IBM focuses on software and services and of course, mainframes are still the top priority.

During Opel's tenure IBM did not simply hold to its traditional marketplaces. It entered new ones but then did not have the expertise to survive. In addition to the PC, the Company moved into Computer Branch Exchanges (CBX) and it acquired the Rolm Company, which made an advanced telephone switch at the time. IBM also bought a piece of Satellite Business Systems and had to sell that when nothing happened. Big Blue also took a small stake in Intel, reportedly to shore up Intel against Japanese competition. It should have taken a larger stake and did something about Intel selling to clone manufacturers.

After he stepped down as IBM's chief executive, Mr. Opel remained chairman until May 1986 and he was a board member until 1993. Mr. Opel passed away on November 2, 2011.

Chapter 21   A Look at John Akers' Years With IBM

From the Book: *Thank You IBM*
Chapter 45 A Deeper Look at John Akers' Years

Opportunity accomplished list had no entries

John F. Akers took over for John Opel as CEO in 1985. By the time Akers took office the cash was all promised to pay for Opel's past adventures. The drawing board Akers had to look at demonstrated that IBM was going to have to do a little scraping and some scrapping to keep itself afloat. Under Opel, the Company decided that it was going to be capacity driven, rather than be like the old IBM which was always supply constrained.

In the Akers years, IBM continued to execute better than any other company in the mainframe product area, but the mainframe marketplace was flat, not growing like the exciting minicomputer, PC and RISC processing areas. Five years of building John Opel's plants had given IBM tremendous production capacity, but the Company had focused on the wrong product areas and it forgot how to sell.

To meet the decreasing demand for IBM PCs, and to meet the new but small demand for the RISC based RT PCs, and to meet the unexpected modest rise in Series/1 sales, IBM did not need the huge amount of manufacturing plant capacity, which post Opel was now ready to come on-line.

It takes a mainframe

While IBM was still counting on mainframes to pull it through, its competitors were making a killing in the markets in which the IBM Company chose not to vigorously compete. As the competition advanced, IBM appeared to lay down and accept its plight rather than fight back. Cosmetic changes and face saving were the order of the day.

Rhetoric, rather than a resolve to innovate and prosper became a hallmark of Chairman Aker's regime. Whereas John Opel had built the farm, John Akers took IBM awful close to buying the farm.

During the 1970's and through 1985, IBM had successfully passed through the Watson years, the Learson years, and the Cary years. In the early 1980's, feeling very good about IBM, to the point of being cocky, then Chairman, John Opel forecast that IBM would be a $100 billion company by 1990. Akers took over in 1985.

From the time Opel gave the word to begin expanding IBM to meet his lofty goals, the Company began to change dramatically, and the words "best customer service possible," and "respect for the individual," began to be used sarcastically by many IBMers who could not explain how the new IBM was in synch with its once venerated mantras.

John Akers is given credit by most IBMers for messing up the IBM we knew. Meanwhile Mr. Akers chose to blame the marketing force for his failure. We were not selling enough!

New IBM hires learned a different culture

In the 1980s, in trying to achieve john Opel's $100 billion dream, IBM began to hire again—lots of new people. But the new hires were treated differently. College culture had changed and the college grads hired by IBM expected something from the Company. They had big-time expectations. When I was hired, I hoped that I could make it and do well in the Company. This new crew expected the Company to give them something whether they earned it or not. They wanted quick returns simply for having joined IBM.

In the 1980's, IBM wasn't sure what it was going to do with its field force, especially systems engineers. Top management no longer believed that it needed to provide top quality support to customers. IBM felt it had nursed its customers into competence over the years. IBM believed that its customers were not willing to pay a premium for any free support included in the price of the product.

IBM Systems Engineers, the folks who helped salesmen know what to sell and helped them sell it, could design a system on a blackboard to get a sale. They then could help the customer implement it exactly as designed. These bright technicians no longer had value in the new IBM world. I was glad that IBM did not know how to fire us all right away but there was a lot of stress knowing that Big Blue would be happy to get rid of us all. It was not comfortable at all working for Akers' IBM but everybody was happy to still have a job with IBM.

In the sixties and seventies, every Systems Engineer had to learn how to write programs. SEs had to get technical to survive. When a customer had a problem with a statement in an RPG or COBOL or Assembler program, a systems engineer would help them resolve it. SEs got good at programming and often fixed their customer's coding problems for free. The more programs customers' wrote, the more IBM equipment they would need to run the programs.

The new IBM never gave new hires the opportunity to mature technically. Instead, they learned how to sell and install packages, and enlist third party help for the technical piece. Some got by merely by knowing how to order large system software. IBM managers were slow to recognize this transition, as the IBM technical force became less and less competent.

A socialized reward system emerged

The Company also lost sight of the purpose of its reward systems. The most coveted award for a Systems Engineer was to be nominated for the Systems Engineering Symposium. Symposiums were awe-inspiring. They were three-day events in a beautiful location. Nominees would hear the best speakers and executives in IBM, and other general interest speakers who were the best in their field.

As a further reward, the attendees would be feted by the best entertainers in the world (Four Seasons, Beach Boys etc.). IBM spared no expense on motivational speakers such as Merlin Olson, Bob Richards, Henry Kissinger, and Walter Cronkite, etc. They were great events. Only the best Systems Engineers in the US would be invited.

In Utica, I watched Nick De Salvo get nominated every year. Nick was tops in Utica, and everybody knew that to take Nick's slot, you had to get as good at your job as Nick was at his. In Scranton, I saw Tommy Vasil and Tony Opalski get the nod every year. I watched what it was that each did and how they did what they did.

Eventually, I too learned how to be a professional and be respected by my customers, IBM management, and my peers. In 1974, after my fourth year with the Company, I was selected and I soon became a regular at the Systems Engineering Symposium.

In the 1980's, because of charitable back to the field type employee programs to save the jobs of displaced IBM plant people, IBM Systems Engineering managers who were not qualified were put in place. My manager for example had never been a Systems Engineer, yet he was charged with evaluating my technical contributions.

These new managers simply were not as good at differentiating talent, abilities, and real accomplishments. They had a tough time understanding who had done what for whom, and why it was significant or insignificant. Moreover, the marketing managers seemed to be controlling the technical action more and more.

Systems Engineers began to be nominated for the Symposium or they would receive large cash awards simply because they had assisted in a sale, not because they had achieved a major technical feat which resulted in a huge sale or a happy customer.

It no longer mattered that an SE had helped a customer achieve a level of technical greatness, which would have been impossible without his or her expertise. It no longer mattered that, thanks to direct SE assistance, customers were making effective use of IBM equipment.

It only mattered that the customer bought a lot of new stuff from IBM. The new SEs quickly learned with these new rules, that technical proficiency was not as important as marketing awareness.

At the same time, as previously noted, with the merging of divisions, reorganizations, back-to-the field programs etc., individuals without the necessary skills, were often promoted to technical managers (SE Managers). If a person had been a manager in a prior IBM position, regardless of the type of position, chances are they would wind up a manager in the field. Since the Company did not want to risk having these folks become marketing managers without having been marketing reps, the SE manager's job was a good dumping spot for them.

For several years before I took IBM's great retirement parachute, I had the non-pleasure of working for a manager who had never worked in a computer division, and who was mostly computer illiterate. Though he was bright and talented, his Office Division background had not prepared him to manage a team of computer technicians.

It is actually a big negative to the whole IBM field system that a person with such a background was able to survive while his technical team was sinking. IBM eventually asked this manager to rank all employees and cut the ones on the bottom. The truth is that in Akers' IBM, as long as somebody was terminated, and IBM no longer had to pay their salary, it did not matter how good of an employee they ever were.

New SE Managers such as mine quickly became politicians in the Company to survive. They could not differentiate the actual accomplishments of their force, since they had never walked the walk or talked the talk. With social skills and hearsay as their major guiding principle, they began to socialize the recognition system. In these bad times, IBM took back 10 or 20% of SE salaries and then gave year-end bonuses and other recognition awards. Some employees got nothing back. IBM managers began to merely split the rewards, regardless of merit, so that "nobody would get upset."

The cause and effect relationship between hard work, accomplishments, and rewards became very broken. SEs with two years' experience, for example, would be sent to the Symposium simply because management believed that "it was their turn."

Akers could not afford Opel

IBM had decided that its technical and marketing direct field force had become too expensive to sustain. Considering its misuse, it is understandable that the Company would reach such a conclusion. It seemed that John Opel's expansion program had made everything too expensive for John Akers.

IBM begins to emulate its poor competitors

Somehow the advanced vision farm in IBM had stopped producing good ideas. IBM was plum out of thoughts on how to keep the organization successful. In desperation, the Company began to adopt a business model used by its less successful competitors from throughout the years. Though this was a bad idea, at least it was an idea.

IBM competitors were always a dime short in how they dealt with their customers and prospects. They had no expensive marketing team with long-term relationships with customers. Instead of using its own staff, IBM's competition franchised their action through distributors. They did not use a direct sales force.

Though IBM at the time was still the leader in the overall computer industry and had gained customer loyalty because of its support structure, the IBM chieftains decided to abandon their formerly successful formula for employees and for customers. IBM began to emulate its competition.

Akers' IBM stopped traveling the high road

IBM has always had a ton of lawyers ready to defend its practices, right or wrong. Before I left, during the John

Akers years, IBM was not a good company, and its lawyers defended the Company's self-serving actions to a fault. I saw some bad decisions by IBM in a number of areas. IBM wanted to get rid of employees, especially older employees who offered the least resistance and who were the most vulnerable.

Akers' IBM squeezed employees and made them feel incompetent in plant and field locations. In this way, Big Blue could thin the ranks by making its employee morale so bad that the people that management were squeezing for *supposed better performance,* would have enough and just quit.

All of their actions during the Akers' years and beyond were not legal but IBM always held the upper hand with its retirement and exodus transition options. I saw firsthand undue pressure on older employees, and other employees who simply happened to be in the wrong place at the wrong time.

Since John Akers was mentioned in discrimination case after case, IBM's lawyers worked to get him a protective court order to block his deposition from being taken in employee action cases. IBM lawyers do not defend regular employees—just IBM executives. John Akers was too important for IBM's continuing business needs to be deposed.

Sometimes it would take a long time for cases to hit the courts. The negative employee policies of today in IBM got their start in the Akers' years. Here are a few stories with that as a backdrop:

Kathy M. Kristof from the Los Angeles Times on August 10, 2003 wrote: "With help from a federal judge, Kathy Cooper has thrown a monkey wrench into the world of corporate pensions. In late July, Cooper, a 53-year-old internal auditor at IBM Corp., won a landmark court ruling that could make it tougher for companies to convert their traditional pension plans into so-called cash-balance retirement plans. U.S. District Judge G. Patrick Murphy, ruling in IBM vs. Cooper, found that the computer giant illegally discriminated against older workers when it switched to a cash-balance plan in the 1990s."

Here's another one: James Castelluccio, a 41-year IBM employee sued IBM in Federal court and won a substantial award. Nothing comes easy when facing IBM, but Mr. Castelluccio had the guts to see it through. This Stamford man claimed that IBM had dismissed him after 41 years because of his age. He is now collecting between $3.5 and $4 million following his federal court trial. The judge said IBM should have been interested in uncovering the truth regardless of whether the employee, James Castelluccio, had taken the severance package or pursued his lawsuit. The judge basically chastised IBM and awarded millions to the plaintiff.

As the story goes, a few weeks before Castelluccio's 60th birthday, his manager Ms. Collins-Smee, in her very first meeting with Castelluccio, asked him his age and if he was interested in retiring. He said he had no interest. The next day, Collins-Smee sent an e-mail to the human resources department saying she wanted to replace Castelluccio and that things were not going well between him and her.

Hey, they had just met! She said that Castelluccio would agree with that point that all was not well. Castelluccio never even knew of this e-mail until the discovery phase of the subsequent lawsuit. As you can see, since Akers, and perhaps before him, IBM did not always play fairly.

IBM decided to defame the employee, make him feel worthless and hope he would cave and take a package as many other beleaguered older employees had done under pressure over the years. The jury deliberated for about a day

and then returned a verdict in favor of Castelluccio.
Sometimes the right thing happens when you take on the
bad guys. In the end, the total of the judgment is between
$3.5 and 4 million.

More recently, Mark Lungariello wrote about another
lawsuit that accuses IBM of age discrimination. The suit
was filed in 2014. Three former IBM employees accused
IBM that they and others were pushed out of the Company
in favor of younger, recent college graduates. This is not yet
resolved. Remember, there are over a million stories in the
Naked City! Here is one more:

Jill R. Aitoro, an Industry Reporter for iSeries Network.com
wrote about this issue on September 17, 2002:   "A band of
laid-off IBM workers in Vermont is pointing fingers at Big
Blue for what they claim to be some fishy practices.
Findings from a study of the June 2002 layoff at the
Vermont Microelectronics division spurred some former
employees to file complaints against IBM for age
discrimination. Another study of the November 2001 layoff
at the same IBM locale revealed nearly identical results."

Is a union the answer for IBM employees?

All during my IBM career, there were no unions at IBM
because employees felt we did not need them. IBM truly
practiced a notion of "respect for the individual." IBM for
the most part was a good company until Akers blatantly
broke the many promises made by the Watsons to loyal
IBM employees. A union sure would have helped hapless
IBMers in the Akers' years.

And, so, today, for the life of me, I have no idea why IBM
employees simply do not organize for self-preservation as
the Company has been changing long-standing practices ad
hoc to save bottom line money. This has had the effect of
harming IBM employees and retirees.

This IBM union is worth a hard look. Here is the Alliance@IBM Local 1701's Statement of Principles. From what I have read, they are a principled organization and they already do a lot of good for IBM employees and retirees:

> *Alliance@IBM/CWA Local 1701 is an IBM employee organization that is dedicated to preserving and improving our rights and benefits at IBM. We also strive towards restoring management's respect for the individual and the value we bring to the Company as employees. Our mission is to make our voice heard with IBM management, shareholders, government and the media. While our ultimate goal is collective bargaining rights with IBM, we will build our union now and challenge IBM on the many issues facing employees from off-shoring and job security to working conditions and company policy.*

I never liked unions when I was with IBM as they have a way of homogenizing all employees into the same soup. I did like how in my time with the Company, there were some good IBM managers who made an attempt to fairly evaluate employees and reward them accordingly with bonuses and promotions.

What recourse would I have had if IBM decided to defraud and fast-talk and chisel its employees with negatives and lawyer-speak, as seems to be happening now? I would have been screaming bloody murder looking for my own lawyer or a good union for sure.

In my twenty-three years with the Company, I met very few IBM employees who were not downright excellent. Working with such sharp people and competing for the spoils of a non-union shop at the time was a lot more exciting for me than getting an 87c an hour raise because everybody else got one.

However, in watching IBM's behavior close hand and through the press over the last few years that I was with IBM and since, I would not trust IBM management today to ever do the right thing for me. IBM managers will gladly rule against any employee even if the accusations are untrue and it may ruin the employee's life. If I were with IBM today, I would surely be a member of this reasonably new Alliance. As a retiree, I have already signed up. For employees, it would help even out a game that today is always won by IBM.

The second unbundling

Whereas the original unbundling of 1969 marked the beginning of the deterioration of the customer / IBM relationship, it hit its all-time low in the last few of the Akers' years (late 1980's—early 1990's.) IBM, not having learned from its mistakes of the late 1960's, again unbundled support from system sales. And, in a move, which made the new unbundling as permanent as the end of the rental business, IBM began to retire or fire (lay off without a possible rehire) its field representatives, both systems engineers and marketing personnel.

In another bold move, IBM also changed its sales model from direct to a distributor-driven channel strategy. IBM's customers of the early 1970s had become outraged by unbundling, after IBM unilaterally announced that the Company was cutting-off free technical support for its products. Likewise, the less trusting, less loyal customers of the early 1990s were similarly outraged.

Unlike the 1970's however, when IBM's customers wanted to complain about the shabby treatment they were receiving from Big Blue, this time, the customers found that there was nobody left home to listen to their complaints other than the competition.

Beginning of the end for IBM's branch offices

Hell bent on separating the customer from the reason they chose IBM in the first place (the best support in the industry), IBM chose a cowardly implementation approach this second time around. Never having forgotten unbundling and the price Buck Rodgers, head of the Data Processing Division at the time, had to pay for his decision, no IBM executive was going to lose anything by *announcing* another cessation of support.

They just did not announce it. They merely eliminated most of the people who populated the local offices. The de-facto result was that IBM customers no longer had any IBMer calling on them. And, nobody in IBM bothered to tell the customer. I am not kidding. I got out as soon as I could under the Individual Transition Option II (ITO II), which was IBM's best deal ever before the axe fell.

For leaving early voluntarily, I got 47 weeks' severance pay; I got paid for all my unused vacation time – over 10 weeks. I got a five year bump to my service from 23.5 to 28.5 years. I was able to receive all IBM benefits, including medical for my wife and family for life. When I reached 30 years from my start date, I began to collect my pension as if I had worked 28.5 years. It was a good deal.

I then opted to take an employment deal at one of my accounts as an inside consultant and professor at Misericordia University. Part of my contract was a lot of time off for outside consulting. I created a consultancy with many of my former IBM customers as my clients. Former IBM Systems Engineers had little trouble finding work.

Ironically, one of my big challenges was convincing customers that IBM had actually withdrawn support. Many had such undying faith in IBM that they could not believe that nobody in IBM had told them how IBM changes would affect them. Their next surprise was when somebody from XYZ distributing called on them and said they were the customer's new IBM representative and showed an IBM business card with their name, IBM's Logo, and XYZ Distributing. IBM had taken a preposterously cowardly way out.

From the customer's perspective, it was as if one day they had a salesman and a technical representative and the next day, not only did they not have an account team, but the team was no longer employed by the IBM Company. They either had taken the retirement incentive or they were fired. If a field employee in systems or marketing had the misfortune of being ranked number "last," regardless of their appraisal rating, they were as good as gone.

Consequences of reneging on customer support

One might ask if it is coincidence that when the Company first unbundled in the late 1960s and early 1970s, IBM's sales took a turn for the worse. The question can be asked again when IBM again unbundled in the early 1990s, and IBM went through some of its worst years ever, losing $16 billion in three years; was it unbundling that created some of the business slump?

From 1991 through 1993, IBM lost money at a staggering rate. No company could endure such record losses. The three year record losses ended in the year in which Lou Gerstner took over as CEO of the Company, when Mr. Akers stepped down. In 1994, IBM began a rebound. Gerstner had reversed many of Akers' practices and IBM stopped its bleeding. The red ink days were over.

Definitely unbundling IBM support from the price of IBM hardware contributed to Akers' and IBM's demise. There was nobody left, who was trained by IBM to ask for a customer order. What company would fire competent sales people who worked on a commission basis when sales were down?

With a poor economy, the depletion of the rental base, and the demoralization and ultimate elimination of many key employees, and the purposeful irritation of the customer base, there was nothing and nobody left to help IBM recover... until Lou Gerstner showed up at the front door.

For his efforts in the major changes which rocked IBM at its very foundation, including the second unbundling, John Akers met a similar fate to that of Buck Rodgers. When Wall Street began to complain about IBM results, Akers was gone.

Ira Sager of Armonk, N.Y., a writer for Business Week, captured some of Lou Gerstner's thoughts on the IBM he inherited in 1993, shortly after Akers' quiet unbundling; his fire sale of IBM divisions, and long-awaited departure:

> One of IBM's most glaring problems, Gerstner concluded, was not its various technology gaffes but that it had basically screwed up relations with its customers. Once famous for blanketing big corporations with legions of pin striped marketing and field engineering troops, Big Blue had become distant, arrogant, unresponsive...
>
> ... Meanwhile, the Company squandered what it had taken decades to build: a position of trust with customers and the ear of top decision makers in corporations... Gerstner saw firsthand how bad things had gotten shortly after joining. When he invited CEOs of major corporations for a technology briefing, [IBM] managers had to scramble to find enough chief executives to fill the 20 slots.

LETS GO PUBLISH! Books by
Brian Kelly: (sold at www.bookhawkers.com etc.).

LETS GO PUBLISH! is proud to announce that more AS/400 and Power i books are becoming available to help you inexpensively address your AS/400 and Power i education and training needs: Our general titles precede specific AS/400 and other technology books.

Great Moments in Penn State Football Check out the particulars of this great book at bookhawkers.com.

Great Moments in Notre Dame Football Check out the particulars of this great book at bookhawkers.com or www.notredamebooks.com

WineDiets.Com Presents The Wine Diet Learn how to lose weight while having fun. Four specific diets and some great anecdotes fill this book with fun and the opportunity to lose weight in the process..

Wilkes-Barre, PA; Return to Glory Wilkes-Barre City's return to glory begins with dreams and ideas. Along with plans and actions, this equals leadership.

The Lifetime Guest Plan. This is a plan which if deployed today would immediately solve the problem of 60 million illegal aliens in the United States.

Geoffrey Parsons' Epoch... The Land of Fair Play Better than the original. The greatest re-mastering of the greatest book ever written on American Civics. It was built for all Americans as the best govt. design in the history of the world.

The Bill of Rights 4 Dummmies This is the best book to learn about your rights. Be the first, to have a "Rights Fest" on your block. You will win for sure!

Sol Bloom's Epoch ...Story of the Constitution This work by Sol Bloom was written to commemorate the Sesquicentennial celebration of the Constitution. It has been remastered by Lets Go Publish! – An excellent read!

The Constitution 4 Dummmies This is the best book to learn about the Constitution. Learn all about the fundamental laws of America.

America for Dummmies!
All Americans should read to learn about this great country.

Just Say No to Chris Christie for President!
Discusses the reasons why Chris Christie is a poor choice for US President

The Federalist Papers by Hamilton, Jay, Madison w/ intro by Brian Kelly
Complete unabridged, easier to read version of the original Federalist Papers

Kill the Republican Party!
Demonstrates why the Republican Party must be abandoned by conservatives

Bring On the American Party!
Demonstrates how conservatives can be free from the party of wimps by starting its own national party called the American Party.

No Amnesty! No Way!
In addition to describing the issue in detail, this book also offers a real solution.

Saving America
This how-to book is about saving our country using strong mercantilist principles. These same principles that helped the country from its founding.

RRR:
A unique plan for economic recovery and job creation

Kill the EPA
The EPA seems to hate mankind and love nature. They are also making it tough for asthmatics to breathe and for those with malaria to live. It's time they go.

Obama's Seven Deadly Sins.
In the Obama Presidency, there are many concerns about the long-term prospects and sustainability of the country. We examine each of the President's seven deadliest sins in detail, offering warnings and a number of solutions. Be careful. Book may nudge you to move to Canada or Europe.

Taxation Without Representation Second Edition
At the time of the Boston Tea Party, there was no representation. Now, there is no representation again but there are "representatives."

Healthcare Accountability
Who should pay for your healthcare? Whose healthcare should you pay for? Is it a lifetime free ride on others or should those once in need of help have to pay it back when their lives improve?

Jobs! Jobs! Jobs!
Where have all the American Jobs gone and how can we get them back?

Other IBM I Technical Books

The All Everything Operating System:
Story about IBM's finest operating system, its facilities; how it came to be.

The All-Everything Machine
Story about IBM's finest computer server.

Chip Wars
The story of ongoing wars between Intel and AMD and upcoming wars between Intel and IBM. Book may cause you to buy / sell somebody's stock.

Can the AS/400 Survive IBM?
Exciting book about the AS/400 in a System i5 World.

The IBM i Pocket SQL Guide.
Complete Pocket Guide to SQL as implemented on System i5. A must have for SQL developers new to System i5. It is very compact yet very comprehensive and it is example driven. Written in a part tutorial and part reference style, Tons of SQL coding samples, from the simple to the sublime.

The IBM i Pocket Query Guide.
If you have been spending money for years educating your Query users, and you find you are still spending, or you've given up, this book is right for you. This one QuikCourse covers all Query options.

The IBM I Pocket RPG & RPG IV Guide.
Comprehensive RPG & RPGIV Textbook -- Over 900 pages. This is the one RPG book to have if you are not having more than one. All areas of the

language covered smartly in a convenient sized book Annotated PowerPoint's available for self-study (extra fee for self-study package)

The IBM I RPG Tutorial and Lab Guide – Recently Revised.
Your guide to a hands-on Lab experience. Contains CD with Lab exercises and PowerPoint's. Great companion to the above textbook or can be used as a standalone for student Labs or tutorial purposes

The IBM i Pocket Developers' Guide.
Comprehensive Pocket Guide to all of the AS/400 and System i5 development tools - DFU, SDA, etc. You'll also get a big bonus with chapters on Architecture, Work Management, and Subfile Coding.

The IBM i Pocket Database Guide.
Complete Pocket Guide to System i5 integrated relational database (DB2/400) – physical and logical files and DB operations - Union, Projection, Join, etc. Written in a part tutorial and part reference style. Tons of DDS coding samples.

Getting Started With The WebSphere Development Studio Client for System i5 (WDSc) Focus on client server and the Web. Includes CODE/400, VisualAge RPG, CGI, WebFacing, and WebSphere Studio. Case study continues from the Interactive Book.

The System i5 Pocket WebFacing Primer.
This book gets you started immediately with WebFacing. A sample case study is used as the basis for a conversion to WebFacing. Interactive 5250 application is WebFaced in a case study form before your eyes.

Getting Started with WebSphere Express Server for IBM i Step-by-Step Guide for Setting up Express Servers
A comprehensive guide to setting up and using WebSphere Express. It is filled with examples, and structured in a tutorial fashion for easy learning.

The WebFacing Application Design & Development Guide:
Step by Step Guide to designing green screen IBM i apps for the Web. Both a systems design guide and a developers guide. Book helps you understand how to design and develop Web applications using regular RPG or COBOL programs.

The System i5 Express Web Implementer's Guide. Your one stop guide to ordering, installing, fixing, configuring, and using WebSphere Express, Apache, WebFacing, System i5 Access for Web, and HATS/LE.

Joomla! Technical Books

Best Damn Joomla Tutorial Ever
Learn Joomla! By example.

Best Damn Joomla Intranet Tutorial Ever
This book is the only book that shows you how to use Joomla on a corporate intranet.

Best Damn Joomla Template Tutorial Ever
This book teaches you step-by step how to work with templates in Joomla!

Best Damn Joomla Installation Guide Ever
Teaches you how to install Joomla! On all major platforms besides IBM i.

Best Damn Blueprint for Building Your Own Corporate Intranet.
This excellent timeless book helps you design a corporate intranet for any platform while using Joomla as its basis.

IBM i PHP & MySQL Installation & Operations Guide
How to install and operate Joomla! on the IBM i Platform

IBM i PHP & MySQL Programmers Guide
How to write PHP and MySQL programs for IBM i